EVOKING SOUND

The Choral Warm-Up
METHOD, PROCEDURES,
PLANNING, AND CORE
VOCAL EXERCISES

James Jordan

Required companion books and videos available from GIA Publications, Inc.

The Structures and Movement of Breathing
(G-5265)
by Barbara Conable

*Evoking Sound: Body Mapping Principles
and Basic Conducting Technique*
"Breathing Sequence" and "Core of Balance" sections
(DVD-530 or VHS-530)
by James Jordan and Heather Buchanan

*Ear Training Immersion Exercises for Choirs:
A Companion to Choral Ensemble Intonation*
(G-6429 and G-6429A)
by James Jordan with Marilyn Shenenberger

Other publications by James Jordan available from GIA Publications, Inc.

The Musician's Soul

The Musician's Spirit

The Musician's Walk

The Musician's Soul: Meditations
by Fr. Bede Camera, O.S.B.,
and James Jordan

*Evoking Sound: Fundamentals of Choral
Conducting and Rehearsing*

The Evoking Sound Choral Series

*Choral Ensemble Intonation:
Method, Ensemble, and Exercises*
Text and video
by James Jordan and
Matthew Mehaffey

*Learn Conducting Technique
with the Swiss Exercise Ball*

EVOKING SOUND

The Choral Warm-Up

METHOD, PROCEDURES, PLANNING, AND CORE VOCAL EXERCISES

James Jordan

FOREWORD BY HELEN KEMP

SUPPLEMENTAL RESOURCES

The Choral Warm-Up Teaching Cards (G-6397-I)

The Choral Warm-Up Method, Procedures, Planning, and Core Vocal Exercises CD (G-6397-CD)

The Choral Warm-Up Core Vocal Exercises: Accompanist Supplement (G-6397-A)

GIA Publications, Inc.
Chicago

**Evoking Sound: The Choral Warm-Up
Methods, Procedures, Planning, and Core
Vocal Exercises** James Jordan

Art Direction/Design: Yolanda Durán

Photography by Eric Kephart. Used with permission.
ZONK ARTS Gallery, 622 South Fifth Street
Philadelphia, PA, www.zonkarts.com
Models Hannah Espiritu, Lydia Espiritu,
Elizabeth Jordan, Katherine Reedman.

G-6397
ISBN: 1-57999-389-3
Copyright © 2005, GIA Publications, Inc.
7404 S. Mason Avenue, Chicago, IL 60638

www.giamusic.com

All rights reserved.
Printed in the United States of America.

Dedication

Dedicated to
   Helen Kemp

This book is dedicated to Helen Kemp. Her teaching and her spirit have inspired countless conductors to use singing to unleash the joy of the human spirit in everyone who has a song. With *Body, Mind, Spirit, Voice* as her mantra, she has inspired everyone with whom she has worked and taught the miracle of the human spirit through singing.

and to
   Frauke Haasemann

Frauke Haasemann, likewise, taught us all that it was truly possible to teach healthy vocal technique to choirs through "tools" that we give them at each rehearsal. But it was her remarkable spirit that remains as our teacher.

Table of Contents

Foreword by Helen Kemp xiii
Acknowledgments xiv
Preface xvi
Introduction xix

PART I   1
MUSIC APTITUDE AND THE CHORAL ENSEMBLE

Chapter 1: Music Aptitude and the Choral Ensemble 2
Developmental Music Aptitude 3
Stabilized Music Aptitude 4
Interpretation and Application of Scores of Music Aptitude for the Choral
      Ensemble 4

PART II   7
THE FOURTEEN PEDAGOGICAL CARDINAL RULES

Chapter 2: The Fourteen Pedagogical Cardinal Rules: A Brief Overview .8
Seating and Its Influence on Laryngeal Position 18

Chapter 3: Philosophy of the Choral Warm-Up: Is a Warm-Up
      Necessary? 20

Chapter 4: The Collective Mentality of the Choral Rehearsal: Abandonment
      of Vocal Responsibility 22

PART III   25
BUILDING VOCAL SKILL

Chapter 5: Building Vocal Skill: A Pedagogical Hierarchy for Choirs . . .26
Pedagogical Ordering 29

Chapter 6: Philosophy of Teaching Techniques 30
Use of Specific and Consistent Terminology as a Strong Pedagogical
      Tool 31
Allowing for Poor Singing Before Teaching 32
Vocal Modeling: Pro or Con? 33
Vocal Curricula 33
Relaxation: Deconstructing Posture Brought to the Rehearsal 33

PART IV
SPECIFIC TEACHING TECHNIQUES

Chapter 7: Alignment and Body Awareness 38

Teaching Alignment Awareness: Employ Body Mapping Principles to
      Re-Educate the Singers 39
Alignment vs. Posture 39
What Is a Body Map? 40
Teaching the Core of the Body: The Six Points of Alignment 41
The Proper Use of Rehearsal Room Chairs 43
Use and Interpretation of the Phrase "Up and Over" 46
Suggested Awareness Reminders 47
Use of Verbal Reminders to Reinforce Awareness 47
The Use of Music and Folders in Rehearsal 47

**Chapter 8: Spaciousness and Proper Vocal Production through the Use of
      the Sigh: Relaxation of the Vocal Tract — Creating Space** 49

Teaching Procedure for the Sigh 50
The "Up Over and Up" Gesture to Reinforce the Sigh 56
What You Should Hear When the Sigh Is Technically Correct 56
Sigh or Siren? 59

Chapter 9: Breathing: Inhalation and Exhalation 60

Inhalation: Remapping the Trachea 61
Breathing: Teaching "Support" or "On the Breath" Singing 63
Steps in Teaching the Breath "Kneading" Exercise 64
Use of Breath "Kneading" Exercise to Document Connection to
      Singing 70
The Pros and Cons of Diaphragm Activity 71
Lip Trill Dangers 71

Chapter 10: Building Resonance 73

Creating General Resonances 73
Specific Resonances 74
The Pedagogical Necessity of Head Tone 76
Choosing the Sequence of Exercises: Begin with Middling the Voice ...76
The Logic of Vowel Closure and Proper Use of the Lips in Closing Vowel
      Sounds 77
Remapping the Lips 79

Listening for Musical Line and Vocalic Flow 80
Life Issues with Musical Line 81
Absence of Love: Normal Illusion 81
Vowel Development Hierarchy 82
Consonants in Vocalization 84

Chapter 11: Vocal Technique "Recipes" 87
Dynamics 87
Crescendo/Decrescendo 88
Range Extension Upward 91
Vowel Modification and Range Extension 92
Range Extension Downward 93
Leaps 94
Legato 95
The Kinesthetic of Vocalic Flow 96
Staccato Singing: Does It Exist for Singers? .97
Martellato 98
Compromise Techniques 98
Teaching Martellato 99
Use of Pointing to Assist in Gaining Textural Clarity 99
Steps for Teaching Martellato 101
Teaching Diction through the Choral Warm-Up 102
Choosing the Appropriate Vowel Color 103
Six-Step Diction Teaching Technique 104
Teaching Pieces That Are Highly Rhythmic 107
Vowel Correction Hierarchy 107
Interdependent Relationship and Pedagogy of the "oo" and "ee"
    Vowels 108
Basic Diction Pitfalls 109

PART V   113
AURAL IMMERSION AND AURAL PREPARATION OF THE CHOIR

Chapter 12: Aural Immersion and Aural Preparation of the Choir 114
Basic Assumptions 115
Pedagogical Sequencing of Immersion Exercises 118
General Teaching Procedure 119
Specific Teaching Procedures for Each Category of Exercises 120

Chapter 13: Blending through Standings and Rehearsal Room Chair Arrangements 122
Pros and Cons of Scattered Quartet Standings 122
Curved Seating Arrangements 123
"Alto in the Front" Seating Arrangement 124
Adaptation of the Modified Seating Arrangement for Treble Choirs ...125
Acoustic Standing Procedure for All Choirs 125
Turning Order Inside Out to Change Sound 130
Acoustical Auditions for Highly Select Ensembles 131
Seating Arrangement for Large SATB Choirs 131
Seating Arrangement for Choirs with Fewer Men 131
Transferring Seating Arrangements from Rehearsal Space to Concert Space 132

Chapter 14: Energizing the Sound of the Choir: A Philosophical Challenge 134
Approach 1: The Dulling World of Our Daily Lives 135
Approach 2: Awareness 136
Approach 3: Bringing a Rhythmic Commitment to the Singing Process 136
Approach 4: Causing Singers to Understand the Miracle of Awe and Wonder 137

PART VI 139
PHYSICAL GESTURE AND KINESTHETIC AS TEACHING TOOLS

Chapter 15: Physical Gestures to Reinforce Choral Warm-Up Principles 140
Pointing 140
Up and Over 142
Heel of Hand on Forehead 143
Finger Toss into Forehead 144
Toss Open Leg Lift 145
Forward Spin 146
Breath "Kneading" Gesture 147
Forward Ball Toss 148
Dipping 149
Body Tip 150
Breath Anchor and Space Umbrella Diagonal 151
Flick and Lighten (Tip of the Tongue "L" Finger Flick) 151

Finger Twirl Over the Head 151
Drooping Hands 151
Resonance Swimming Cap Peel 151
High and Forward Finger Wand (the "oo" Magnet) 157
Tossing Clap 157
Hand Dab for Energy 159
Hand Smoothing Gesture 160
Congealing Sound Mixing Gesture 162
Linguine Pull Gesture 166
Upward Cheekbone Brush 168
Sound Rolling Gesture (for *piano* and *pianissimo* dynamics) 169
Consonant Wisp Gesture 170
Upward Toss (for sound weight reduction) 172

Chapter 16: An Application of the Work of Rudolf von Laban to Propel Musical Line 175
Rudolf von Laban 179
Philosophical Basis of the Work of Laban 180
The Laban Effort Elements: Flow, Weight, Time, and Space 181
Experiencing the Efforts in Combination .182
Application of Laban Efforts in Combination to Musical Phrase and
  Direction of Musical Line 189
Summary 191

PART VII 193

BUILDING CONSISTENT TEMPO SKILLS THROUGH THE CHORAL
WARM-UP

Chapter 17: Strategies for Teaching Rhythm 194
Muscle Coordination Development 195
Rhythmic Response to External Music vs. Internal Musical Impulse . . .197
The Structure of Rhythm and Its Relation to Rhythm Pedagogy 197
Natural Body Response to Rhythm: The Foundation for Understanding
  Rhythm 198
Layers of Rhythm Audiation 199
The Role of Consistent Tempo in Music Performance 201
Using a Metronome to Establish Communal Kinesthetic Tempo 202

PART VIII — 205
CONSTRUCTING YOUR WARM-UP

Chapter 18: Rehearsal Planning Template 206
Warm-Up Planning Template 208
Warm-Up Planning Template: Completed Example 213

PART IX — 219
TROUBLESHOOTING CHORAL ENSEMBLE PROBLEMS AND SUGGESTED SOLUTIONS

Chapter 19: Troubleshooting Chart 220

PART X — 235
THE CORE VOCAL EXERCISES: HARMONIZED MELODIC FORMULAE FOR WARM-UPS

Chapter 20: The Core Vocal Exercises 237
Introduction by James Jordan 237
    Instructions for the Conductor 238
Introduction by Marilyn Shenenberger 240
    Basic Rules for Accompanists 242
Choral Warm-Up Exercises: Quick Overview .245
Choral Warm-Up Exercises: With Accompaniments 250

PART XI — 305
THE CHORAL WARM-UP TEACHING CARDS AND CORE VOCAL EXERCISES

Bibliography and Resource List 308
About the Authors 324
Index 327

Foreword

James Jordan possesses multiple gifts of communication. As a choral conductor, he communicates through physical gesture, facial animation, mental intensity, and spiritual zest as he evokes inspired sound from his singers.

Another of his gifts is the ability to communicate the principles of vocal techniques and choral concepts through the *written* word. Dr. Jordan has a way of transforming the facts of empirical knowledge by using new and creative terminology, often challenging the reader to reconsider accepted teaching philosophies and methods.

In his constant search for vocal and choral excellence, Dr. Jordan has created and shared volumes of valuable idealistic and practical information. One of his goals, it seems to this writer, is to inspire the *artisan* to become the *artist*. I believe my own personal mantra also embraces the concepts so eloquently written in Dr. Jordan's volumes:

> Body, Mind, Spirit, Voice....
> It takes the *whole* person to sing and rejoice.

Helen Kemp
June 2004

Author's Note: One may note that this volume is dedicated to Helen Kemp. Helen was unaware that I was going to dedicate this book to her when she wrote this foreword.

James Jordan

Acknowledgments

So how does a clarinetist write a text on vocal technique for choirs? Due to many serendipitous events, I was taught the art of teaching choirs to sing from some of the best teachers of the past thirty years. And as always, my students played the major role in this text. The work of many teachers over the years and the willingness of many choirs to serve as a laboratory for this pedagogy culminated in a book of this nature.

My choirs at Lewisburg High School and The Westminster Chapel Choirs from 1991–2002 have been my best teachers. The fact remains that during my years at Lewisburg, those incredible students who were brave enough to study with me taught me much about the vocal instrument. While all deserve to be listed, there are some whose work and patience with me deserve mention: Rita Richard, Marc Persing, Margaret McClure, Christie Pyper, Jack Milne, Christopher Hettenbach, Brownyn Hettenbach, Rae Jean Hartley, Bernard Kunkel, William Lumpkin, Christopher Ross, Steven Freed, Eric Kroner, James Younkin, Mark Pyper, Douglas Goshorn, Kelli Gilbert, John Mckeegan, Cynthia Miedel, Tina Groover, Lindy Groover, George Miller, Christopher Delbaugh, Martha Strickland, and Tim Dougherty. Thomas Gallup, in particular, provided a standard for vocal teaching that I still reflect upon today. Two gifted students who have gone on to major careers as performers also played significant roles: John McVeigh and Lynn Eustis.

My years at Temple University were blessed with gifted singers, friends, and classmates. They sang in my choirs, and their very musicianship taught me volumes. In particular, Marietta Simpson and Evelyn Simpson, through their musicianship and spirit, had a profound impact on my future teaching and me.

My work early in my career with Frauke Haasemann, Helen Kemp, William Trego, and Nancianne Parella formed the basis of much of my thought. My friends Constantina Tsolainou and Sabine Horstman also served as models for what I consider to be great vocal "teachers" of choirs. The gifted and dedicated voice faculty members at Westminster have unknowingly served as my teacher over these many years, and ALL deserve my thanks. And the magic of being at Westminster has challenged me to find the best ways to arrive at a beautiful vocal product. Westminster faculty members who have been inspirations for me over the years have earned my deepest thanks: Lorna MacDonald, Anne Ackley Gray, Zahava Gal, Laura Brooks Rice, Elem Eley, Margaret Cusack, Thomas Faracco, Julia Kemp, Guy Rothfuss, Marvin Keenze, Scott McCoy, Charles Walker, and Sally Wolf.

Marilyn Shenenberger began as a student and presently assists me in my work with The Westminster Williamson Voices. Her strengths as both musician and accompanist can be seen in the core vocal exercises written for this book and the valuable aural immersion exercises written for *Ear Training Immersion Exercises for Choirs* (GIA, 2004). Her work has been crucial to the writing of this book. Thanks to Eric Scott Kephart, who created the photographic images for this book and continues to support my work and life in countless ways. Thanks to Catherine Payn of the Bucknell University faculty, who has served as both a resource and a sounding board over the years.

And thanks to GIA for the continued support of my work and ideas. Edward and Alec Harris continue to support not only my work but also the work of so many other music educators who strive to improve how we teach. And deepest thanks to my editor, Linda Vickers. Texts such as this require not only editorial expertise but also an ability to grasp the material and maintain an overview of the entire project. Her efforts have made this project a reality. Her eye for detail and her very spirit have nursed this long and, at times, tedious project through some difficult challenges. She is an invaluable colleague in this work, and that work is reflected on all the pages of this volume. Without her, the book you are about to read would not have been possible.

And finally, to the now thousands of students over the years who have endured my lectures and biases on this subject that I love, my deepest thanks for your encouragement and feedback.

James Jordan
Yardley, Pennsylvania
December 2004

Preface

I remember a number of years ago hearing a lecture by Craig Denison, who at that time was working with choirs at The American Boychoir School. He remarked that teaching young singers on a daily basis was both frightening and daunting. The basis of his premise was that he always had a type of litmus test for his teaching. He always thought, in regard to the teaching of vocal technique, that if he made a mistake, it might take thousands of dollars in vocal study to correct bad pedagogy in later years. That is most likely true.

As a clarinetist, I felt totally inadequate teaching vocal music, although I loved the genre so much I decided that I could "learn" how to teach vocalists to sing in a similar way as I was taught as an instrumentalist to teach the instruments. Little did I realize that unlike the instrumental field, there were few, if any, materials written to prescribe a method fused with techniques that could accomplish that goal. For the past twenty-five years, this has been one of my missions.

A voice teacher friend has often remarked to me in various subtle ways about the amount of vocal "damage" that is inflicted upon singers through a choral experience. I tend to agree with her. While it is dangerous to refer to a paradigm that both exaggerates and groups all choral directors into one narrow category, I do believe that our profession has not paid as much attention to this very important aspect of our teaching. Why? Because teaching people to sing can be challenging.

The most valuable book prior to 1970 had been William Finn's *The Art of the Choral Conductor*. An unfortunately small group read that book, yet it laid out many important ideas that have strongly influenced my thought. Granted, during the past twenty years, many gifted teachers, especially in the area of children's choirs, have made invaluable contributions to that end: Helen Kemp, Doreen Rao, Henry Leck, John Cooksey, Jerry Blackstone, Jean Ashworth Bartle, Kenneth Phillips, Lynell Jenkins, Judy Willoughby, Constantina Tsolainou, Lynn Gackle and, of course, Frauke Haasemann. Each has presented to all of us an invaluable perspective. Any conductor who is interested in teaching choirs to sing should know all these materials in addition to the materials presented in this volume. There never can be enough techniques or ideas about teaching. I encourage you to read their materials if they are unfamiliar to you.

My concern is for all of us to tend the vocal health of our choirs, regardless of their level of development. Aside from giving the gift of music to the people we teach, we are charged with a higher responsibility: to give them vocal "tools"—as Frauke Haasemann often said—to use for the rest of their lives to enjoy the miracle of singing. I have seen many conductors, many of them with considerable reputations, conduct choirs with "beautiful" sound but with grave long-term consequences for the vocal health of the singers in those ensembles. This primarily stems from a lack of pedagogical knowledge that is overtaken by an overriding sense of musicianship. Many times musical objectives overshadow vocal integrity and human dignity. Those choirs sing with a contrived and manufactured vocalism that is somehow willed to be in tune. Many also believe, often unknowingly, that choral "blend" is achieved by sublimating all voices and spirits into an obeying whole.

For those conductors who have realized the importance of pedagogy and have pursued it as a science mixed with love, their choirs sing with a remarkable resonance, brilliance, and spontaneity that is unmistakable. Moreover, many of them understand that great choral singing is not about the manipulation and repression of the human spirit. They also understand that great pedagogy is always counterbalanced by love and care at all times in the rehearsal/teaching and performance process.

There is nothing more motivating for singers as singing in an ensemble that "sounds." The sonic gratification is what has attracted so many of us to this incredible art. But to be teachers of choirs carries great responsibility. We need to be partners with voice pedagogy. We need to learn as much as possible about teaching people to sing, and we need to love those people at all times in the process.

So, that is our charge. I present here the summary of my thought and experience the past fifteen years. It is my viewpoint, and there are certainly others. However, the standard I believe we all should accept is to teach voice in such a way that allows our singers to sing freely at all times so their spirits can take them on a journey through the great music we have been given. It is a daunting and noble task, but I believe it is achievable.

Despite all the knowledge we can acquire about singing technique, there is another danger: the danger that we hide behind how much we know. The more we know sometimes equates itself to good teaching. Quantity of techniques should not be our only goal. Quantity without counterbalancing love will never achieve great choral singing. I would like to end with a quote by the great American clergyman, William Sloan Coffin, which seems to place all in perspective.

So Socrates was mistaken: it's not the unexamined life that is not worth living; it's the uncommitted life. There is no smaller package in the world than that of a person all wrapped up in himself. Love is our business. (p. 12)

William Sloan Coffin
The Heart Is a Little to the Left

Introduction

> Choral conductors, even more so than teachers of singing, are divided in their opinions concerning vocal technique. Some refuse to employ any means to build voices. Either they consider such procedures to be unimportant, or they are afraid to use an exercise that is related to the singing process. Sometimes choral directors cloak their own ignorance of the singing mechanism by dealing directly with the interpretative elements in a score and, thus, avoid any approach to the vocal problems of the individuals in a chorus. There are also those conductors who insist upon using only the techniques learned from a favorite teacher. These are applied regardless of the nature of the problem or the desired solution. Finally, there are some who, without an orderly plan of procedure, utilize a great number of vocalises, devices, and methods taken from many sources with the desperate hope that the tone of their chorus somehow will show a marked improvement. (p. 8)
>
> Howard Swan
> *Choral Conducting Symposium*

Since first studying with Frauke Haasemann in 1978 at Westminster, I have spent a good portion of my career studying and applying the vast amount of pedagogical information she shared and left to us all. One of the frustrations I had as an instrumentalist turned choral conductor was the surprising lack of pedagogical materials available to help conductors teach choral ensembles via a group setting and within a group dynamic.

The intervening years have seen the publication of many materials. As I teach my seminars in Group Vocal Technique and Choral Ensemble

Vocal Technique, it is clear that conductors at all levels need a streamlined and concise resource that will keep important pedagogical Group Vocal Technique principles at the forefront of their thinking. This text is a manual to serve as an overview of the most important Group Vocal Technique principles and to serve as the medium for new principles that have been developed in recent years.

Exercises that should be used to aurally prepare the choir are presented in *Ear Training Immersion Exercises for Choirs: A Companion to Choral Ensemble Intonation* (GIA Publications, 2004). Teaching principles for teaching beginning aural literacy through the choral ensemble warm-up are detailed in that volume. This volume contains exercises with the objective of teaching vocal technique. The reader will notice similar exercises presented in both texts. The reason for this is to encourage teachers to select exercises that strengthen listening and exercises that teach vocal technique. Those two concepts should **not** be commingled. The use of similar exercises are used in the hope of showing that a wealth of exercises is not necessary as long as the pedagogical purpose is clearly defined.

This book will hopefully serve as a concise summary and trusted guide for the sequential vocal development of any choir, regardless of their level of development. Frauke Haasemann believed in a patient, pedagogically sound, and consistent process to give the choir the vocal "tools" needed to sing the music. I hope this book will serve as a crystallizing and concise "quick reference" guide so your warm-ups can become the pedagogical "heart." of your rehearsal. This book builds upon the concepts presented in *Group Vocal Technique* (Hinshaw Music, 1991). However, I have made some adaptations that are reflective of my thought and experience over the past fifteen years, and I have incorporated the requests of hundreds of workshop participants for materials that deal with newly found teaching techniques.

This volume will attempt to redefine and further clarify the pedagogical order of the choral ensemble warm-up. It will present a concise series of exercises that can be used with specific vocal technique objectives that can be used as a starting point for those using these materials for the first time. The exercises, I believe, form the core of a collection of exercises that can teach the essentials of vocal technique to the choir. After these exercises are mastered, then other exercises can be added. However, I believe these exercises should form the "core" of any choral ensemble's vocal training. I would also like to note that these exercises are appropriate for choirs at any age or level of development. Chronological age is of no consequence. Vocal experience level is the determining factor when selecting musical materials to be used in the warm-up period.

My thought has significantly changed on the use of accompaniments in the warm-up. For many years, I preached the value of the *a cappella,* unison warm-up. Given my thoughts concerning *Choral Ensemble Intonation* (GIA Publications, 2002), I now firmly believe it is necessary to provide a rich harmonic background, or aural immersion, for meaningful music learning to take place. Hence, this volume is a slight departure from the materials I have designed in the past. It is a sharp departure in the pedagogical road of ensemble listening and hearing. I believe that **both** vocal technique and aural awareness must be reinforced during warm-up. I have also come to believe that the dynamic of the choral ensemble presents a powerful environment for the teaching of aural skills. Unison singing devoid of harmonic richness breeds inattentive listening, which can be detrimental to the learning of performance literature. However, warm-ups that are harmonically well conceived and that provide a steady diet of harmonic richness can enhance music listening while teaching essentials of Choral Vocal Technique. (When I refer to "Choral Vocal Technique," I am referring to the principles developed with these clarified objectives.)

In this volume, I detail the "method" for teaching vocal technique as I believe it should be approached within the choral rehearsal. For each technical step of this Choral Vocal Technique, I present a concise "recipe" of teaching steps necessary for the specific vocal technique and, in each section, a vocal exercise that I believe is efficient in teaching the technique. These are what I refer to as the "Core Vocal Exercises." These core exercises should be used first and then supplemented with other exercises collected by the conductor that can further define and perfect vocal technique.

The Choral Warm-Up Teaching Cards are available separately from the publisher (GIA, G-6397I). These cards are concise duplications of the pedagogical materials presented in each chapter. I have found that persons beginning to use these materials benefit from having these pedagogical "reminders" to take into rehearsal with them.

PART I
MUSIC APTITUDE AND THE CHORAL ENSEMBLE

Chapter 1
Music Aptitude and the Choral Ensemble

> More often than not, we talk of things that we scarcely know, we often discuss things of which we have no knowledge, and in reality we are often ignorant of things that we think we love. (p. 96)
>
> A teacher must develop first consciousness, second memory and tools, and third expectation. (p. 68)
>
> Nadia Boulanger
> *Master Teacher*

Wouldn't it be wonderful if you really knew how well your choir could hear? Notice that I said "hear" and not "read." For some reason, the musical achievement of a choral ensemble has always been based on how well the ensemble could read, but the focus should be on how well a choir can hear. It is hearing—and the acuity of that hearing—that determines the difficulty of literature a choir can perform. In teaching a choir, beginning with the warm-up, one should not handicap one's teaching by making subjective assumptions about the choir's musical abilities.

There are several serious pedagogical dangers that lurk if subjective opinion is the only factor used to assess musical ability. First, performance achievement is usually not an indicator of how one hears. Music aptitude, by definition, is the potential for one to hear music. Whether that potential is realized is an equal product of pedagogy and objective information.

The miracle of choral singing is that choirs are composed of groups of persons. Since music aptitude is normally distributed in any musical population, within any group there most likely is a normal distribution of highly aurally talented individuals combined with numbers of moderately talented and minimally talented individuals. It must be realized that their musical aptitude may or may not be defined by their performance abilities. Performance ability is a subjective evaluation, which should not occupy a place in one's pedagogical plan. Conductors who assume their choirs are not aurally talented waste much rehearsal energy. They over-teach, which guarantees the choir will never realize its true performance potential. Instead, choral conductors who know the listening abilities of their choirs can turn the pedagogical table on the choir and place most of the responsibility for music learning on the singers. Imagine the luxury of selecting literature based upon two factors: (1) the vocal demands of the piece and (2) the aural demands of the piece.

For the past twenty years, there have been highly accurate measures available to choral conductors for the measurement of music aptitude. While there are many music aptitudes, we can efficiently measure only two: (1) the ability to hear and **remember** pitch and (2) the ability to hear and **remember** rhythm. It is those two basic musical skills that define one's music aptitude. They are also the same skills that will define and accurately predict the performance level of any choral ensemble.

Developmental Music Aptitude

Prior to age nine, music aptitude is in a state of flux. Depending upon one's aptitude, experience, and influences, one's level of music aptitude can be maintained or may decline. If one is denied either by educational design or by environmentally musically enriching circumstances and instruction, then music aptitude will decline. Conversely, if music aptitude is nurtured with a diet of environment and instruction, the music aptitude level that one is genetically endowed with can be maintained. In other words, you have the same musical potential you had at age nine!

Throughout this period of "aptitude maintenance," there are measures of developmental music aptitude that can be administered. The *Primary Measures of Music Audiation* (PMMA) (GIA Publications) and the *Intermediate Measures of Music Audiation (IMMA)* (GIA Publications), by Edwin E. Gordon, are highly reliable, objective measures of developmental music aptitude that will yield both a rhythm score and a tonal score based upon a large normative sample across all ethnic and socio-economic backgrounds. The tests can be administered to large groups of students, regardless of language reading ability. The tests come with all necessary information for scoring and accurate interpretation of scores. PMMA is a more basic form of the test, designed for populations with limited exposure to music and/or music instruction. IMMA should be administered to populations where either music experiences or music instruction has been enriched in some way.

Stabilized Music Aptitude

After age nine, music aptitude stabilizes. Because abilities have stabilized, another music aptitude test must be administered. The *Advanced Measures of Music Audiation (AMMA)* (GIA Publications), also by Edwin Gordon, is similar to PMMA and IMMA, and requires approximately 25 minutes to administer. A tonal and rhythm score will be provided to the teacher. Because music aptitude has stabilized, this test need only be administered once after age nine.

Interpretation and Application of Scores of Music Aptitude for the Choral Ensemble

There are many ways to employ the use of music aptitude assessment scores in one's choral ensemble teaching. The manuals that accompany these tests detail the interpretation of the percentile scores. Note that on these particular tests, scores at or above the 50th percentile are considered to possess music aptitude. Applications of the percentile scores are as follows.

1. **To determine the aural hearing potential of each section of the choir.** If you take the tonal score of the measure and then take the average of all the scores in a section, you will have a general idea about the hearing potential in that section.

2. **To assist with the selection of choral literature.** Once you have determined the tonal and rhythm average of each section, you will have a sense of what your choir can hear. Regardless of their music reading ability, you can select music based upon hearing difficulty. This difficulty has been determined by research and is detailed in *Choral Ensemble Intonation* (GIA Publications, 2002). Difficulty is directly related to harmonic sophistication and mode (i.e., Dorian, Phrygian, etc.).

3. **To determine appropriate rehearsal techniques for your ensemble.** After you have determined the hearing potential of each section, you can begin to make decisions about the "what" and "how" of teaching. It follows that sections with high music aptitude should always sing in tune and learn parts on first hearing period. However, if a section is lower in music aptitude, that does not mean the singers cannot learn to sing in tune or learn the part in harmonic context. It just means the teacher

will need to be careful in the choice of rehearsal procedures and be patient with the section's progress.

You will find that the use of these applications will maximize the productivity of your choral ensemble and focus your rehearsal procedure because you know what your choir is capable of singing.

For youth choirs and school choirs, there should be no question as to their use. However, their use within the church setting must be carefully considered. Church choir members, often set in their ways, typically become intimidated by such measures. In those situations, measurement should only be used in the most comfortable working situations for the conductor. Generally, one should avoid testing in new situations or employment early in one's career.

PART II

THE FOURTEEN PEDAGOGICAL CARDINAL RULES

Chapter 2
The Fourteen Pedagogical Cardinal Rules: A Brief Overview

> Finally, there is a need in vocal education for a well-rounded, multi-faceted approach to singing that combines the usual concern for artistry with accurate knowledge of the singing process. Instructors who adhere to unbendable methods are unfair to aspiring singers. It behooves teachers to derive their techniques of teaching from comprehension of fundamental principles rather than from processes learned by rote that becomes more distorted as it moves through succeeding generations of teachers and singers. (p. 2)
>
> Maribeth Bunch
> *Dynamics of the Singing Voice*

In doing warm-ups and studying their unusual alchemy of pedagogical material and human interaction, there seems to be a potent and strong common denominator in all warm-ups that are musically successful. Most of my conclusions are based upon much observation, especially of Frauke Haasemann and her students, particularly Sabine Horstmann and Constantina Tsolainou.

Choral conductors must realize that the quality of the warm-up determines what will transpire for the rest of the rehearsal. Poor warm-ups lead to poor rehearsals. Remarkable as it may seem, I have found that the omission of **any** of the steps presented on the pages that follow creates a negative, snowballing pedagogical effect on the rest of the rehearsal, which reduces or halts music learning. Experience has also shown that it is unwise to proceed into the literature portion of a rehearsal until all of the "cardinal rules" have been accomplished.

The general pedagogical "core" of a warm-up is not a complicated matter. It does, however, require a tutorial persistence on the part of the conductor, and a loving insistence on the part of the conductor that these points be achieved. **Provoking** and **evoking** are equal partners in this process! When analyzing the great work of many conductors, there seems to be one overriding principle—that of dogged adherence to a set of pedagogical principles, which achieves long-term and dramatic vocal growth. This is certainly true in great studio teaching. The same should be the case in teaching choral ensembles as well.

A narrow and concise set of vocal objectives is absolutely necessary when dealing with singers of limited experience. This narrow set of objectives must be presented in a pedantic order for the vocal principle to be applied. As one of my music theory professors always said, "System is comfort." Many persons I have observed use the warm-up to bombard the choir with vocal techniques in the hope that such a bombardment will, through quantity, improve their technique. While some vocal technique can be acquired through such pedagogical bombardment, healthy, long-term vocal growth occurs through carefully chosen and pedagogically narrowed materials at the beginning stages of vocal development.

In each warm-up, there are certain pedagogical issues that must always be accomplished. Regardless of the length of the rehearsal, these objectives must be accomplished if the rehearsal is to be vocally healthy.

The Fourteen Pedagogical Cardinal Rules

1. Deconstruct posture brought to the rehearsal.
2. Realign and employ Body Mapping principles to reeducate the singers.
3. Create and reinforce awareness at all times.
4. Use the sigh to create space and diagnose vocal issues.
5. Inhalate and exhalate.
6. Generate resonance.
7. Sing on the breath at all times.
8. Be certain all sounds are rhythmically vital.

> 9. Use physical gesture to reinforce the singing process and body awareness.
> 10. Be certain all sounds are spacious, high, and forward (SHF).
> 11. Reinforce pitch awareness.
> 12. Use a repeated exercise as "home." Always use **Core Vocal Exercises.**
> 13. Use the same warm-up sequence in planning each warm-up.
> 14. Make certain that regardless of the exercise, the position of the larynx remains low and relaxed.

What follows is a brief summary of pedagogical principals for each of the points above. A "mini-chapter" is devoted to each point. For further in-depth pedagogical information, consult the resources listed in the bibliography of this book.

Rule 1 DECONSTRUCT POSTURE BROUGHT TO THE REHEARSAL.

When singers enter the choral rehearsal, they bring with them their personal accumulation of poor "posture" acquired throughout the day. In the beginning of the choral ensemble warm-up, the initial step is to perform activities that will take the posture in a direction of deconstruction—breaking apart the muscular rigidity and postural incorrectness, and moving to a state of body alignment borne out of a balanced and aware skeletal system.

Rule 2 REALIGN AND EMPLOY BODY MAPPING PRINCIPLES TO REEDUCATE THE SINGERS.

Body Mapping is a principle that has been championed by Barbara Conable in her application of the principles of Alexander Technique. The reader is referred to her books (listed in the bibliography of this text) for further information and explanation. Based on my experience, Body Mapping and the conductor's understanding of its principles are the most important aspects of choral ensemble pedagogy. An understanding of Body Mapping allows for a pedagogical unlocking of all other aspects of vocal technique. In fact, depending on the singers, this information alone creates bodies that will sing better, making it possible for a choir to sing well.

Rule 3 CREATE AND REINFORCE AWARENESS AT ALL TIMES.

In addition to kinesthetic and tactile awareness, singers need full experience of their own emotions and the emotions inspired by the music they're singing. All this inner awareness, together with auditory and visual information, is called inclusive awareness. Inclusive awareness contains all relevant information in the moment the information is needed. Inclusive awareness is a rich and pleasurable state of being, one of the reasons people love singing so much. As a bonus, inclusive awareness and an accurate Body Map are effective proof against problems that plague singers, truly protecting singers over a lifetime. (p. 13)

Profound embodiment is also the key to ensemble. Singers' continuous, intimate, often intense awareness of their own bodies (sensations, movements, and emotions) is the ideal condition for feeling and responding to each other and to the conductor. Then a chorus is a chorus and not just a collection of individuals singing at the same time. The many choral conductors who have helped their singers regain full body awareness as they sing are surprised and delighted by the terrific difference embodiment makes in the quality of the singing. (p. 14)

Barbara Conable
The Structures and Movement of Breathing

If one wanted an overall objective for great choral ensemble teaching, it would be to create **inclusive awareness** at all times during the rehearsal process and performance. While many of us teach various aspects of vocal technique, I think our pedagogical shortcomings lay in the fact that we do not reinforce and incorporate that teaching with awareness. Without such awareness, pedagogical information recedes as other musical matters take hold. It is possible for pedagogical information to be made part of one's inclusive awareness. The key to that process is to link the pedagogical concept with a kinesthetic. If choral ensemble teaching has had any shortcomings, it has been its inability to kinesthetically link pedagogical information to a body kinesthetic, or rather, a kinesthetic awareness.

The reason for this is the fact that, heretofore, musicians have always believed they have only five senses to work with as teachers. The fact is that there are **six** senses, the sixth being kinesthesia, narrowly defined as the feeling of the body when engaged in musical performance. For musicians, **hearing** and **kinesthesia** must be their most important senses. With every rehearsal, a reprioritizing of the senses must take place if vocal technique is to be not only learned but also easily recalled.

While it may seem difficult to teach a type of inclusive awareness that includes kinesthesia, it is actually relatively simple. Being aware is a state that is easily achievable once we understand that the world creates in us a state of unawareness. Unawareness can be countered by simply calling persons into a state of awareness by asking them in varying ways if they are aware of themselves. Simplistic as it sounds, this call to awareness is a powerful pedagogical force and is the key to long-term retention and recall in the choral rehearsal. Body Mapping, aural awareness, listening, and feeling are all components. It is the responsibility of the conductors to contemplate ways to constantly call their choirs into a state of awareness that is not fleeting, but rather prolonged and alive.

Rule 4 USE THE SIGH TO CREATE SPACE AND DIAGNOSE VOCAL ISSUES.

The use of what is referred to as the "sigh" is one of the most valuable pedagogical tools available to the choral conductor in determining the overall health of the vocal mechanism. Its power as a diagnostic tool should not be underestimated. A complete understanding of how to teach proper technical execution of the sigh is at the core of all vocal instruction for the choir. In other words, if the choir cannot execute the sigh in a vocally correct way, then consequent vocalism will suffer. Most importantly, a choral warm-up cannot and should not proceed until the sigh is correctly executed.

Rule 5 INHALATE AND EXHALATE.

Perhaps more than any of the other cardinal rules, this rule is most often taken for granted. It is assumed that inhalation and exhalation are natural occurrences that do not need to be taught. While singers naturally respirate and understand breathing for life, they lack an understanding of breathing for singing. In every warm-up, inhaling and exhaling exercises must be done so singers readapt their breath mechanisms to accept the air into their bodies so the singing process can take place in a healthy fashion.

Once again, the use of Body Mapping is of primary importance in reinforcing and creating correct inhalation/exhalation in singers. This can only be accomplished, however, after body alignment has been taught and reinforced, as well as reinforcing how air enters the body (like a wave that moves from top to bottom). Later in this text, procedures for teaching inhalation and exhalation will be detailed. Remember that before any phonation can take place, inhalation and exhalation exercises must be performed. Also remember that singers bring with them whatever tensions they have acquired during the day. The warm-up should attempt to purge those acquired patterns and reinforce the correct Body Maps for inhaling and exhalating.

It might be helpful to think of this part of the warm-up as the creation of a container for the breath. Alignment creates the container, and inhalation and exhalation allow filling of the container. Singers need to practice filling and emptying the container at the beginning of each rehearsal.

Rule 6 GENERATE RESONANCE.

Of all the steps in the warm-up process, this is the one that is most often either missed or performed at the wrong point in the pedagogical sequence. I have found that if this step is not taught and achieved at its appropriate point in the warm-up process, then the vocalism for the rest of the rehearsal becomes unruly and, at times, unusable. Many conductors attribute this to a "bad day." Initial generation of resonance through activation of the resonators creates the raw materials for all vocalism that is to follow.

At this stage of the warm-up, it is important to understand the pedagogical imperative contained in initial resonance vocalises. So important is this step that it can never be missed and must always occur in the warm-up **after** inhalation and exhalation and before any phonation takes place in the rehearsal. If this step is omitted, singers will begin singing with the resonances they have used in their speaking voices all day. Not only are those resonances insufficient sound "fuel" for the singing process, but there needs to be a transition between speaking and singing resonances. In vocal terms, the conductor must be assured that sufficient head resonances (head voice) have been activated. Without that activation, the singing will lack vibrancy and color, and there will be no dynamic variation in the music performed.

Rule 7 SING ON THE BREATH AT ALL TIMES.

One of the conductor's primary responsibilities is to ensure that singers are singing "on the breath" at all times. Regardless of the age of the choir, this rule is often broken. The reason is simple. Conductors are not trained to listen for the differences between a sound that is off the breath and one that is on the breath. Singing off the breath usually causes other choral problems, such edgy, harsh sound; loud singing; pitch problems; and lack of dynamic flexibility, especially within a *piano* dynamic. With an understanding of basic pedagogical processes to teach supported singing, this objective is easily achievable.

Rule 8 BE CERTAIN ALL SOUNDS ARE RHYTHMICALLY VITAL.

Rhythmic vitality in a choral sound is related not only to technical aspects of sound production but also to human elements that are brought to the production of the sound. In fact, more often than not it is the human elements that cause choral sound that is not rhythmically vital. Rhythm is the by-product of an energized, alive human being who is aware of his or her human condition. It is that awareness which provides an aural clarity and distinctive brilliance to the sounds being sung.

Along with inclusive awareness, human commitment to the task at hand energizes the sound more than any specific vocal help. When the spirit is aware and energized, the breath carries that energy through the vocal instrument. Once again, the conductor must be aurally aware of choral sounds that are not rhythmically vital and call the choir into awareness. This cardinal rules has more spiritual implications than any of the other rules. Connection of the singers to themselves and the music will most likely energize a dull sound. Conductor creativity and aural vigilance are important components in this process.

Rule 9 USE PHYSICAL GESTURE TO REINFORCE THE SINGING PROCESS AND BODY AWARENESS.

Within a choral ensemble, it is important to remember that a major pedagogical problem for the conductor is the abandonment of vocal responsibility by those in the choir. **The psychological nature of the choral ensemble creates a dynamic where individual vocal responsibility is inadvertently abandoned.** Through the use of various physical gestures suggested later in this book, reinforcement and accountability for important vocal concepts can easily be accomplished in a non-intimidating way. While specific pedagogical suggestions are given for each of the gestures, feel free to be creative and combine gestures as necessary.

Additionally, the use of physical gesture coupled with vocalizing can continually encourage use of the entire body as a part of the singing process. A constant reinforcement of total body awareness is one of the keys to success in achieving vocal health within a choral ensemble.

Rule 10 BE CERTAIN ALL SOUNDS ARE *SPACIOUS, HIGH,* AND *FORWARD* (SHF).

The remedy to most choral ensemble problems rests with this important vocal premise. At all times, vocal sounds must be spacious, high, and forward. The result of such vocalism is a bright, brilliant, and resonant sound where the pitches of the notes being sounded are clear and distinct. The sound must also be spacious. A sound that is spacious (see "Teaching Procedure for the Sigh" in Chapter 8) possesses a roundness and fullness of tone that is aurally distinguishable from a sound that lacks space (i.e., small, pressed, airy, and lacks freedom and vocal color). By being aurally vigilant at all times for sounds that are spacious, high, and forward, you will avoid many pitch problems.

Rule 11 REINFORCE PITCH AWARENESS.

A series of accompanied "core" vocalises are presented in this volume. In *Choral Ensemble Intonation: Aural Immersion Exercises for Choirs* (GIA Publications, 2004), a detailed rationale is given for the justification of the use of harmonically rich exercises, which underpin the unison singing of the choir.

For years I was taught—and believed—that choirs could be taught to hear better through unison singing. Hence, my warm-ups and "part teaching" were done unison, often with a skeletal piano accompaniment. I now have found through experience that a choir's aural literacy grows exponentially through the supplying of harmonic materials at all times. One's "harmonic surroundings" provide many aural clues for context that are quite powerful;

not to provide such surroundings allows for rampant aural speculation on the part of the singers. Harmonic context is everything. Harmonic context provides many aural links for musicians by providing context for what is being heard. The power of that context has been underestimated in the design of musicianship materials, especially those written for choral ensembles. Consequently, it is important that the harmonic surroundings of the unison exercises be considered as a central pedagogical component for the warm-up.

Throughout the process of learning what a choir actually hears, I have also marveled at the power of the dominant function note in any mode. The sounding of the dominant gives immediate aural organization to the musical materials so they can be learned and understood. Its power cannot and should not be underestimated. While the sounding of the resting tone provides some beginning aural information and begins to focus the ear, it is only when the dominant is sounded in alternation with the resting tone that the syntax of the tonality is aurally identified and organized in the performers' ears.

Consistent with those two points—(1) the importance of harmonic immersion at all times and (2) the aural organizational power of the dominant and resting tones—materials have been written for this text that incorporate these pivotal ideas into the accompaniments of the core vocalises.

Rule 12 USE A REPEATED EXERCISE AS "HOME." ALWAYS USE CORE EXERCISES.

An important pedagogical technique is the use of the "home" or core exercises in the construction of the choral warm-up. Without the use of such exercises, it is difficult for the conductor to ascertain the vocal progress or readiness of the singers. It is even more difficult for the singers to self-assess their vocal readiness for the rehearsal. It is perhaps this last point that is most important to realize.

A repeated exercise or exercises provides and aural and a vocal kinesthetic "benchmark" for singers. The use of repeated exercises allows both the choir and the conductor to accurately assess singing readiness on a given day. Those exercises can also note vocal progress and overall vocal health. In cases where progress and vocal health have declined, the path necessary to restore the choir to those places should be clear to the conductor. It is important to use such benchmark exercises to build vocal accountability into the warm-up process.

Rule 13 USE THE SAME WARM-UP SEQUENCE IN PLANNING EACH WARM-UP.

One of my professors in graduate school constantly repeated the mantra "System is comfort." There is an immense amount of truth in that statement. The success of any teaching—and, for that matter, any method—is inherent in its structure. People will learn most any material as long as that material is presented in a logical, coherent order. It is also of huge pedagogical benefit, a type of systemic comfort, if that material is always presented in the same pedagogical order each time it is presented.

Obviously, decisions concerning teaching order are serious ones. For inherent in those ordering decisions is a distillation of much pedagogical wisdom, opinion, and bias concerning what should be taught first, second, and so on. These decisions should never be taken lightly. The most successful conductors and teachers have made pedagogical decisions and have never swerved from the path they have chosen. Robert Shaw always prepared a piece the same way. The piece was always taught in layers. Pitch and rhythm were anchored via rhythmic count singing. Text was added only after an intense amount of count singing. Mr. Shaw always followed this procedure. Aside from the fact that he developed potent rehearsal techniques, he decided early in his career on a method for teaching a piece of music.

Later in this volume (see Part VIII), a template is presented for the design of every choral warm-up. Strict adherence to this template is highly encouraged, as it was developed after many years of practical experience in the choral rehearsal room. "Cut and paste" the exercises in this book into their appropriate pedagogical slots in the template. Feel free to add other exercises from other sources. However, you are strongly encouraged to use the corpus of exercises presented in this volume as the "core" of your teaching. Only after those exercises have been mastered should you add other exercises. Make certain, however, that those exercises are sung with an aurally rich accompaniment whenever possible.

Rule 14 MAKE CERTAIN THAT REGARDLESS OF THE EXERCISE, THE POSITION OF THE LARYNX REMAINS LOW AND RELAXED.

Aside from ensuring that the vocal sound is always spacious, high, and forward, the other overriding principle for healthy vocal production is the maintenance of a low and relaxed position for the larynx. Many vocal problems have their genesis in vocal mechanisms that are in a high position. Pressing and muscular tension are usually present in such a situation. In fact, because of the collective group mentality, choral ensembles usually breed this problem because of body unawareness that becomes part of the singing process if it remains unchecked. Constant aural vigilance is necessary to prevent this serious vocal problem.

What is the sound of a high larynx? Pressure, tension, a lack of spaciousness in the sound, dull or thin vocal resonance, and "hardness" in the sound are some of the aural danger signs. Overall, there is a lack of freedom in the vocal tone. The conductors must train their ears to be aware of vocal sounds that are not free and beautifully resonant. They must decide for themselves what a free and brilliant sound is, and then be aurally vigilant that it is present at all times. The most efficient remedy for laryngeal distress is the use of the sigh as a relaxing prescriptive to vocal tension. Also remember that this type of damaging vocal tension is a by-product of life experiences throughout the singers' daily routines.

Viewed this way, the choral warm-up gains incredible importance. Left unchecked, laryngeal tension can only be made more severe by a choral rehearsal! It must be the objective of the conductors to maintain a low and relaxed laryngeal position throughout the choral rehearsal. It is also important to teach a type of laryngeal awareness to the choir (i.e., the feeling of what it is to sing with a larynx that is low and relaxed). In a choral situation, much of this can be accomplished by simply asking the choir to listen to everything else except themselves. By using this, a release of tension automatically occurs.

Seating and Its Influence on Laryngeal Position

Perhaps choral conductors who do not use seating within the choral ensemble as a prescriptive unknowingly cultivate more vocal tension and consequent long-term vocal ills. Seating can and does create an environment for healthy singing. Contrary to popular usage, many of the seating arrangements employed by choral conductors acoustically create situations that breed vocal problems. Seating arrangements that have singers placed in "blocks" are dangerous, as singers unknowingly raise their larynx position because of the overabundance of resonance around them. Larger voices tend to develop many vocal tensions in such arrangements because there is not an acoustical freedom that encourages free singing. Smaller voices, likewise, develop tensions because they begin to over-sing to "compete" with the glut of vocal sound around them.

Regardless of the size of the choir or its level of experience, it is important to seat sections in single rows across the width of the choir. Further, the optimal arrangement for vocal freedom within a choral ensemble is to seat singers in four rows—and only four rows, regardless of the size of the choir. The larger the choir, the more the four rows should curve toward a three-sided box.

Fourth row ⟶ **tenor**
Third row ⟶ **baritone and bass**
Second row ⟶ **soprano**
Front row ⟶ **alto**

Use of this seating arrangement creates an environment for free singing and greatly reduces the probability for laryngeal tension that is created by most choral ensemble seating arrangements. For other voicings of choirs, a seating arrangement should be used that is as close to this model as is possible.

Chapter 3

Philosophy of the Choral Warm-Up: Is a Warm-Up Necessary?

> Sound Pedagogy rests upon starting right and upon gradual progress. (p. 23)
>
> William J. Finn
> *The Art of the Choral Conductor*

It is important to be clear on two points concerning the choral warm-up: (1) the purpose of the warm-up and (2) what should be taught during the warm-up.

The first question that is usually asked is whether a warm-up is necessary. Many conductors, teachers, and church musicians feel that because their rehearsal time is so short, a warm-up is not necessary or possible. Regardless of the length of the rehearsal, a comprehensive warm-up (as described in this book) is of the utmost importance. In fact, it is the most valuable part of the rehearsal. Done well, the warm-up can pre-determine the success of the rehearsal. It should contain two important overall elements:

1. Preparing the vocal instrument for correct and healthy singing; and

2. Providing aural instruction, aural orientation, and musical aural literacy for the choir, separate from the literature being taught in the rehearsal and yet intimately related to the tonality of the materials being taught.

This text will not deal with the second part of the warm-up. *Ear Training Immersion Exercises for Choirs* (GIA Publications, 2004) addresses that part in detail.

What must be understood is that choral singers bring a vocal instrument to rehearsal that, in all likelihood, has worked in its speaking voice all day. The primary role of the warm-up is to make a transition from speaking voice to singing voice—that is, to provide a transition from vocalism for speaking to vocalism for singing. If this transition is not made, choirs will sing with the vocalism they use for speaking. Use of the wrong resonances of the apparatus breeds vocal damage and creates numerous choral ensemble problems (e.g., pitch, diction, etc.). Stated even more strongly, it is impossible to have a productive and beneficial choral rehearsal without this vocal preparation. Most problems within a choral rehearsal are not rooted in musical issues, such as pitch, rhythm, etc. If there are such issues, they must be dealt with separate from the vocal issues. Readiness of the voice for singing is the most important objective of any choral warm-up.

Warm-ups need to be conceived within a rigid philosophy of what needs to be done to accomplish such a task. Remember that there are many things that can be vocally accomplished within the warm-up. Conversely, there are certain vocal issues at more advanced stages of development that can only be accomplished in the voice studio on a one-on-one basis. However, basic vocal health and good basic usage are achievable in every choral warm-up. Thought of another way, the warm-up can and should provide the basic "tools" of good vocalism. Those tools, once taught, are then constantly and consistently reinforced with every warm-up. The pedagogical power of such a procedure should never be underestimated. Contrary to popular thought, the warm-up is not intended to "warm up" the voice. Rather, the objective of the choral warm-up is to establish, reestablish, and reinforce the basic elements of good singing in every rehearsal.

Chapter 4

The Collective Mentality of the Choral Rehearsal: Abandonment of Vocal Responsibility

> The singer uses his body to sustain life and cultivate his art. He can never escape from himself, for his physical life either furthers or hinders his artistic life. A good singing teacher and choir director will utilize activities from everyday life as well as natural and acquired capabilities of the body for development of his artistic work. On the other hand, the experience and demands of the artistic life will influence the everyday life of the singers.... (p. 2)
>
> Wilhelm Ehmann
> *Choral Directing*

Abandonment of vocal responsibility is not as easy as it appears. One would think that if basic vocalism were taught, then it would transfer from rehearsal to rehearsal. It does not. Choirs experience group amnesia, which sets in when several or more singers group themselves into a choir. Voice teachers for years have leveled the charge that choirs do vocal damage to singers. Under most circumstances, they do. The reason for this is because the responsibility for singing well is not placed on the shoulders of the singers but rather is assumed by the conductor. The conductor's philosophy must be to place all of the responsibility for good singing on the singers.

Understand that the dynamic of the choral rehearsal breeds vocal irresponsibility and, hence, a plethora of serious vocal problems. There is a vocal unawareness that begins to creep in at the beginning of each choral rehearsal. As the rehearsal progresses, this vocal unawareness grows to the point where serious musical problems develop within the rehearsal. Group numbness with regard to singing overtakes any sense of individual vocal integrity. A well-designed warm-up serves as a vaccine to these phenomena. Conductor awareness of this abandoning of vocal responsibility will translate into a dramatic change in the dynamic of the choral rehearsal. Viewed another way, the choral warm-up reestablishes and reinforces good singing habits. The choral rehearsal, in turn, should be transformed into a series of rehearsal procedures, with the objective of placing **all** the responsibility for good singing clearly with the singers.

PART III

BUILDING VOCAL SKILL

Chapter 5
Building Vocal Skill: A Pedagogical Hierarchy for Choirs

Choral conductors, even more so than teachers of singing, are divided in their opinions concerning vocal technique. Some refuse to employ any means to build voices. Either they consider such procedures unimportant, or they are afraid to use an exercise that is related to the singing process. Sometimes choral directors cloak their ignorance of the singing mechanism by dealing with the interpretative elements in a score and thus avoid any approach to the vocal problems of an individual in a chorus. There are also those conductors who insist upon using only the techniques learned from a favorite teacher. These are applied regardless of the nature of the problem or its desired solution. Finally, there are some who, without an orderly plan or procedure, utilize a great number of vocalizes, devices, and methods taken from many sources with the desperate hope that the tone of their chorus somehow will show a marked improvement. (p. 8)

Howard Swan
Choral Conducting Symposium

Students should be alerted that there are no mysteries regarding the technical aspects of singing. The teacher who regards the technical work of singing as shrouded in mystery inadvertently admits to a lack of information on the physical and acoustic nature of the vocal instrument. Singing appears to be a kind of magical process to this person, and the technique of singing is an idiosyncratic structure built on intuition and trial and error. This explains the technique-mystique teacher's resistance to detailed information regarding the functional aspects of singing. How can one serve as priestess or priest if the mystery is taken away? (p. 211)

Richard Miller
The Structure of Singing

The previous section detailed overall pedagogical principles. These principles are to be applied to all categories in this section. It cannot be emphasized enough that an overall aural vigilance is necessary on the part of the conductor for there to be a state of vocal health with the choral ensemble.

Method is central to all efficient and enduring teaching. Method also contains a combination of bias and experience on the part of the person who writes the method. The "list" or method below may not, and probably is not, the method by which the studio teacher would teach voice. Many times, that method is strongly dictated by the individual being taught but is overseen by broad pedagogical brushstrokes that are at the philosophical underpinnings of the teacher providing the instruction. Good teaching is pedagogically biased teaching, whether in the studio or in the choral ensemble. The routes may be different because of the teaching situation; however, there must be a pedagogical direction and a hierarchical decision concerning how vocal skill should be taught. Choirs need vocal "tools" (i.e., vocal technique that is built in a logical and consistent process). A potpourri approach to choral training does achieve results, but it is neither healthy nor efficient over the long term. A "road map" is necessary.

The "map" or method presented here is based upon firsthand experiences and trial and error over the years, as well as input from numerous voice teachers who are both teachers and conductors. It provides an overriding structure for the logical teaching and building of healthy vocal technique within a choir.

Choral Ensemble Pedagogical Hierarchy

Relaxation

Alignment and Body Awareness

Relaxation of the Vocal Tract: Relaxing the Jaw, Tongue, and Lips

Creating Spaciousness (Use of the Sigh)

Breathing

Exhalation and Inhalation

Support

Resonance

General Resonance

Specific Resonance

Vowel Development Hierarchy

Register Consistency

Dynamics

Crescendo/Decrescendo (Messa di Voce)

Range Extension Upward

Range Extension Downward

Leaps

Legato

Staccato

Martellato

Diction Teaching Principles

Pedagogical Ordering

The pedagogical breakdown is shown on the previous page. **The order within the first section is non-negotiable.** The skills in that section are hierarchical and must be taught in that order in every warm-up. Regardless of the length of the warm-up, these skills must always be reviewed and awakened each time.

The pedagogical order in the **second section** is suggested, as there may be subjective opinion and debate concerning the order within that box. Regardless of the order, those skills and techniques must be taught to the choir. The order is dependent upon the skills the choir brings to the ensemble. For vocally inexperienced choirs, this is the necessary pedagogical order. For more experienced choirs, the order may vary.

The **third section** stands alone because those principles should be taught independently. Diction principles can be prepared in the warm-up, but the application of diction occurs when texts are fused to musical materials. Further, this box deals with the techniques for teaching diction to a choir via the choral rehearsal.

What follows are teaching techniques or "recipes" for each of the categories. While there are many techniques for the teaching of all these elements, those that I have found most efficient in a choral ensemble are presented in this text. The essential teaching steps of those techniques are set apart from the text in boxes. The material in those boxes is reprinted on the index cards that accompany this volume. These cards can be carried into the rehearsal to remind conductors of the basic principles involved with a specific technique.

After mastering these techniques and understanding the objectives for each level, feel free to supplement teaching techniques you believe to be useable to broaden the pedagogical base you employ.

Chapter 6
Philosophy of Teaching Techniques

It is clear to anyone who has worked with choruses of both "amateur" and "professional" voices that well-taught voices can make better choral sound than untaught or badly taught voices. The teaching of voice has to be one of the most difficult and complicated of musical endeavors. You can't see the voice, can't touch it, you frequently have to depend on someone else even to hear it. One can only be grateful to those who undertake this remote and complex task, and who teach it as a means of musical expression rather than self-exhibition. (p. 6)

Robert Shaw
"Letters to a Symphony Chorus"
The Choral Journal (April 1986)

Each singer has a different physiognomy and, therefore, a slightly different sense of focus. This precludes a teacher being able to direct a tone to a specific place such as "behind the front teeth," "in the nose," and "in the sinuses." As a student achieves a certain amount of vocal freedom and coordination of the various parts of the vocal mechanism, as well as a good mental concept of the sound he should be making, proper focus will result. (p. 96)

Because the vocal tract is so complex anatomically and acoustically, many problems about sensation and vocal quality remain unanswered. There is questionable evidence that in singing, the vocal tract should be free to respond dynamically by being spacious and without constriction, and the tone should be properly focused; and the singer who bends his efforts to these ends will almost certainly be rewarded with a noticeable improvement in vocal quality. (p. 99)

It would be hard to find a voice teacher who recommended singing with a closed throat. "Open the throat" is almost as frequently heard as "Support the voice," "Sing on the breath," or "Place the voice." These expressions have the potential for inducing malfunction in singing because they are imprecise. Just as the singer must concretely understand how the tone is "supported" (how the rate of breath emission is determined), so must the singer know what to experience as "the open throat." At best, subjective expressions can be but vague indicators of specific concepts. Such adages can mean many things to many persons. Vocal pedagogy could probably take a major step forward if these and other subjective terms were replaced with, or augmented by, more exact language. (p. 58)

Richard Miller
The Structure of Singing

Use of Specific and Consistent Terminology as a Strong Pedagogical Tool

Efficient and effective teaching is a science of exacting language. So, too, great pedagogy is a result of exacting decisions by teachers concerning the language used with students. One must make decisions to label vocal experiences and singing sensations in the choral rehearsal with a single and, if possible, unique term. There can be a real imminent danger when pedagogical terms are tossed to the choir without clear definition as they relate to a vocal experience. Too many vocal terms not only makes the rehearsal inefficient, but it hopelessly confuses the beginning singer.

The general rule of thumb is **"Experience first and label immediately after the experience."** One should never embark on a vocal concept in the choral rehearsal by explaining first. The adage "talk less" is one that should be carefully observed. Throughout these materials, exercises are presented for teaching purposes. Once the student has correctly experienced the vocal concept, it should immediately be labeled with a term carefully chosen by the conductor. In every repetition thereafter, the same term should be used; no other term should be introduced, even if the meanings are interchangeable. This specific use of terminology empowers both the teacher and the content. Language, then, is used as an accurate and efficient device for instant recall of pedagogical concepts. Efficient and spare language is the key to influential choral ensemble teaching. Many "images" may, and should, be brought into the rehearsal process. However, similar images for the same concept must be labeled with the same term—and no other. One adage that comes to mind is that children can learn anything provided it is logical. For both adults and children, that logic must be supplied by a lean and accurate vocabulary that has always been introduced with powerful sensations and singing experiences.

Allowing for Poor Singing Before Teaching

Another important concept in choral ensemble teaching is that teachers must allow the choir to experience the vocal concept incorrectly before teaching begins. This is also a secret to great teaching. Much pedagogical "pay dirt" is wasted by teaching first before the choir has sung. Allow the choir to sing as they are, almost like a pretest. After they have made an incorrect or improper sound, then begin teaching.

Choirs learn what something is by what it is not. By allowing them to experience an incorrect sound and then immediately experiencing the correct sound, they will feel and hear the difference. When that happens, the teacher's work is, for the most part, done. All the teacher needs to do is accurately label that experience with the proper specific verbiage for later recall again and again!

Vocal Modeling: Pro or Con?

A word needs to be said about vocal modeling. Some of us are great singers, and some of us are not. If you are a skilled singer, always model first before attempting to explain specific vocal concepts. You may save yourself valuable rehearsal time, especially with young singers. If you are not a vocal performer, model to the best of your ability! I have found choirs to be extremely forgiving and kind! They will extract from your modeling what is good, and they always ignore what is not so good! While one should not rely solely on vocal modeling in teaching, it is a valuable tool in the teaching process.

Vocal Curricula

There are many approaches to performance curricula for school programs. Many curricula are built around a prescribed list of performance literature or a prescribed approach or method for the teaching of musical skill. Without doubt, an approach to the teaching of music literacy must be used. However, the other part of the curriculum must be a sequential method to the teaching of vocal technique. Essentially, a choral curriculum should be a reflection of the table of contents for this book. Faculties must make decisions on a consistent methodology, from beginning choirs to the most advanced choirs. Choirs often never realize their vocal potential because as they move from teacher to teacher, valuable pedagogical time is spent as the singers learn to translate from one pedagogical language to another. In the process, there is a loss of vocal technique that is hopelessly lost in the translation process. Literature should be the teaching material of any curriculum, but it should never be the exclusive content of the curriculum.

Relaxation: Deconstructing Posture Brought to the Rehearsal

When singers enter the choral rehearsal, they bring with them their personal accumulation of poor posture and body tensions acquired throughout the day to that point. In the beginning of the choral warm-up, the initial step is to perform activities that will take the posture in a direction of deconstruction: breaking apart the muscular rigidity and postural incorrectness and moving the choir to a state of body alignment borne out of a balanced and aware skeletal system.

Rehearsal Room Suggestion:

Create the possibility for constructive rest before the rehearsal.

To begin the "personal responsibility" portion of this process, it might be helpful to have several Swiss exercise balls in the rehearsal space. If singers arrive early, they should be encouraged to use the balls as a relaxation tool. There are many activities that can be done on these balls, but the most valuable is the "drape." The singers should drape their body over the ball appropriate to their body size and lay in that position for several minutes. Such an activity allows for a natural lengthening of the spine and a refreshed body for singing. Once done, this tends to be addictive for the singers! It encourages early arrival at rehearsals! Barbara Conable uses the term "constructive rest" to describe this activity.

What are these activities? On the next page is a list of descriptive activities that can be creatively varied according to the conductor's wishes and skills. Be creative and develop variations on these themes. Remember that you should never repeat an activity from rehearsal to rehearsal. Repetition breeds unawareness!

Deconstruction of Posture Brought into the Rehearsal

Stretching

Stretching utilizes all extremes of movement: bending, reaching, rotating, swinging, etc.

Playacting situations

Vignettes that ask the choir to act out life activities that employ the above points: imitating skiing, painting, rowing a boat, riding a bike, hanging wash, cooking, packing books on a bookshelf, etc. Such activities not only serve to deconstruct poor posture, but they can reawaken a sense of fantasy that is necessary for the music-making process. Such activities can also serve to begin to expand awareness of the body that is so important to the singing process.

Massaging

Have the choir turn to the right or left and massage each other across the shoulders, and then gently "pummel" with the fleshy part of the hands on either side of the spinal column.

PART IV
SPECIFIC TEACHING TECHNIQUES

Chapter 7
Alignment and Body Awareness

The singer uses his body both to sustain life and to cultivate his art. He can never escape from himself, for his physical life either furthers or hinders his artistic life. A good singing teacher and choir director will utilize activities from everyday life as well as natural and acquired capabilities of the body for development of his artistic work. On the other hand, the experiences and demands of the artistic life will influence the everyday life of the singers. (p. 2)

Wilhelm Ehmann
Choral Directing

The purpose of Body Mapping is to provide a context for vocal technique rather than the technique itself. Vocal technique varies greatly across styles of choral singing, but context for each style is the same. Body awareness, an adequate and accurate Body Map, and freedom from tension serve the members of a jazz choir as well as they will serve a cathedral choir or a gospel choir, though the members are singing with different techniques. (p. 13)

Profound embodiment is also the key to ensemble. Singers' continuous, intimate, often intense awareness of their own bodies (sensations, movements, and emotions) is the ideal condition for feeling and responding to each other and to the conductor. Then a chorus is a chorus and not just a collection of individuals singing at the same time. The many choral conductors who have helped their singers regain full body awareness as they sing are surprised and delighted by the terrific difference embodiment makes in the quality of the singing. (p. 14)

Barbara Conable
The Structures and Movement of Breathing

Teaching Alignment Awareness: Employ Body Mapping Principles to Re-Educate the Singers

Body Mapping is a principle that has been championed by Barbara Conable in her application of the principles of Alexander Technique. The reader is referred to her books listed in the Bibliography of this text for further information and explanation. In my opinion, the most important aspect of choral ensemble pedagogy is Body Mapping and the conductor's understanding of its principles. An understanding of Body Mapping allows for a pedagogical unlocking of all other aspects of vocal technique. In fact, depending on the singer, this information alone can create a body that will sing better, thus enabling the choir to sing well without this information.

Alignment vs. Posture

Many of us were taught either by design or experience that the cue word for all things concerning body usage was **posture**—the "P" word! Conductors should abandon the use of that word in their warm-up rehearsal vocabulary for a simple reason: the use of the word "posture" will recall every image of body alignment the singers have acquired throughout their life—most, if not all, of which are incorrect for singing. A primary role of the choral warm-up is to provide a new mental paradigm that will form the foundation for healthy vocalism. The word that should be employed for this newly taught and discovered body awareness is **alignment.**

What Is a Body Map?

Our Body Maps are our physical self-representations. We literally map our own bodies with our brains, that is, we conceive neurally what we're like (structure), what we do (function), and how big we are (size). We map our whole bodies in this regard, and we map their parts. If our Body Maps are accurate, we move well. If our Body Maps are inconsistent with the reality of our structures, we do not move well. Singing is movement, and its quality is as determined by our Body Maps as the quality of our walking is. Fortunately, inaccurate or inadequate Body Maps can be replaced with accurate and adequate Body Maps. All that is needed is information and attention to information. Human beings are naturally self-correcting, and our Body Maps are no exception. (p. 13)

Barbara Conable
The Structures and Movement of Breathing

The study of the science of somatics has provided us with compelling information concerning the power of the brain in determining the use and misuse of the body for many of life's activities, including singing and the singing process. Basically stated, somatics tells us that if a person's Body Map is incorrect, that person will use his or her body only as he or she perceives it. The Body Map is the acquired mental "picture" of the correct function and structure of the body. This is a powerful pedagogical statement, which has profound and far-reaching implications for how choirs should be taught and how they learn with consequent implications for the choral rehearsal.

Body Mapping can best be described using the old adage that "a picture is worth a thousand words." Body Mapping includes mental maps for **body size, structure,** and **correct usage.** If a Body Map of a person is incorrect, incorrect body usage will be the result. However, once a body map has been corrected and reinforced, it remains corrected forever—a simple and powerful concept that has been ignored in the pedagogy of the choral rehearsal. Incorporation of this principle profoundly changes the pedagogical depth of the warm-up process and the entire direction of the choral warm-up.

Teaching the Core of the Body: The Six Points of Alignment

After the activities that try to "deconstruct" the poor postural habits of the day, a portion of each rehearsal must be spent to reconstruct alignment. Initially, this activity must include teaching that provides for new Body Maps. In later stages of the evolution of the ensemble warm-up, you must then only reinforce and call into awareness the new Body Maps. As Barbara Conable so beautifully puts it, you must use the choral warm-up to give your choir a "piece of the truth"—the alignment truth—in each rehearsal.

Included in this part of the instruction are only the pedagogical objectives for teaching the six points of alignment. For specific teaching instruction, the reader must watch the DVD or video, *Evoking Sound: Body Mapping Principles* (GIA Publications, 2001). The principles should then be taught to the choir in the identical fashion and with the same vocabulary that is used on the video. To assist with the teaching and reinforcement of this material in its initial stages, every member of the choir should be given the diagram below with six gummed stars or notebook reinforcements.

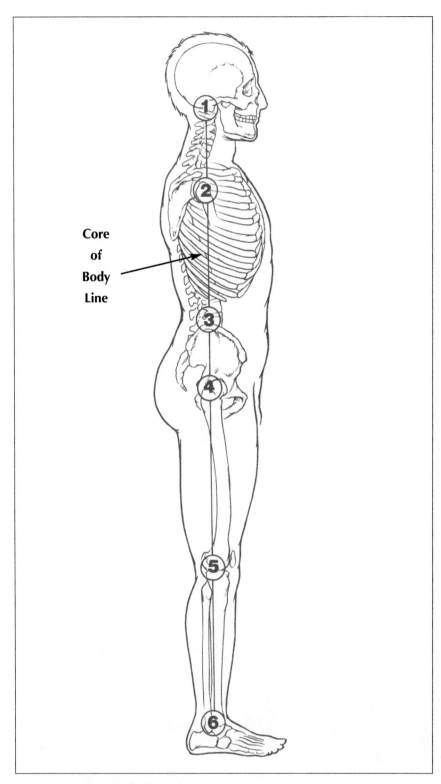

Figure 1 Six Points of Alignment

The Proper Use of Rehearsal Room Chairs

Most chairs in choral rehearsal rooms, unfortunately, are not designed to encourage good alignment. However, with a simple instruction or two, most chairs can be rendered useable.

1. When the choir members sing, have them place one leg back and under the chair. This will ensure a more correct alignment of the core of the body, specifically, the pelvis.

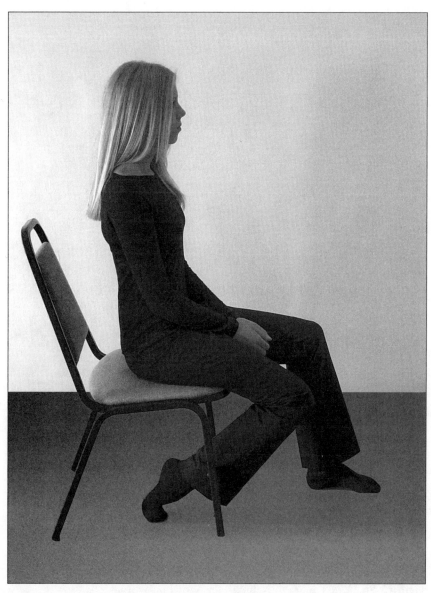

Figure 2 Correct Use of Rehearsal Room Chair

2. Make certain chairs are of the correct height. Many of the chairs in choral rehearsal rooms are stackable. It is important, if possible, to adjust chair height by stacking chairs according to the height of the singer. Most chairs are designed for an average height singer (5′6″ to 5′10″). For shorter singers, a box or hymnals may be used to avoid dangling legs that do not contact the floor. For taller singers, chairs can be stacked accordingly. The rule of thumb for correct height is that the thigh and shinbone should form a 90-degree angle when correct.

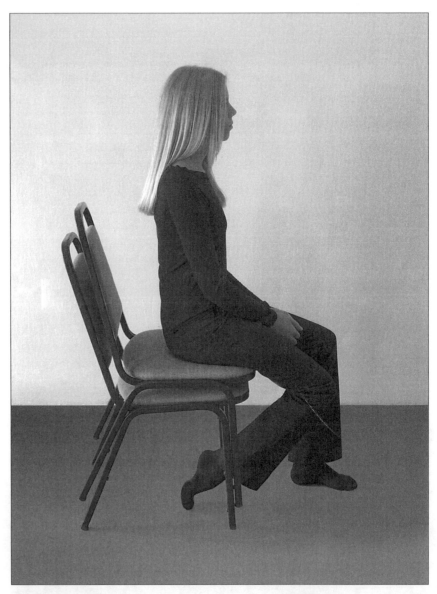

Figure 3 Stacking Chairs to Achieve Proper Chair Height

As demonstrated on the *Evoking Sound* video, as each of the points of balance are explained and mapped, a star or notebook reinforcement should be placed on the point of balance that was taught. This activity, although simple, ensures that the Body Map was correctly acquired. The points of balance that are demonstrated on the video, which must be taught or "re-mapped," are presented below. The order of these points is different from the video to reflect an alignment in order based on what I have found to be the most inaccurately perceived and important points of balance to the "lesser" points of balance. All points of balance must be properly mapped for alignment to be correct and for a total body awareness to take over.

Six Points of Skeletal Balance

Correct Map of the Hips
(the balance of the upper half of our body over the legs)

Correct Map of the A/O Joint
(the balance of our head on our spine at the center)

Correct Map of the Pelvis: The Core of the Body
(the balance of our thorax on our massive lumbar vertebrae at the center)

Correct Map of Shoulders
(the balance of our arm structures over our spine at the center)

Correct Map of the Knees
(the balance of our knees at the center)

Correct Map of the Feet
(the balance of our bodies on the arches of our feet at the center)

What is the **feeling** of being aligned? This standard process is the one I use, almost without exception, in each rehearsal. After reviewing the points of balance:

1. Ask the choir to lean forward. Ask them what they feel. Tension in the lower back area?
2. Ask the choir to come to center, to a place where they feel that **no work is being done.**
3. Ask the choir to lean backward. Do they feel tightness or tension?
4. Ask the choir to return to center where **no work is being done.**

When alignment is correct, the body is in balance. It always will feel as though **no work is being done.** That feeling is the goal of an accurate map of skeletal balance or core points of balance of the body.

Rehearsal Room Suggestion:

Because of the power of visuals that can assist this process, hanging anatomical pictures of the six points of balance around the rehearsal room is helpful for both teaching and reinforcement. It is also helpful to have an anatomical model of the entire skeletal system or just an anatomical model of the spine and the pelvis in the rehearsal room. In the initial stages of the introduction of this material, pass the anatomical model around the room. Such visual aids are virtually indispensable for younger choirs!

Remember that after the introduction of the six points of balance to the choir, these points must be reinforced in **every** rehearsal.

Use and Interpretation of the Phrase "Up and Over"

One hears the phrase "up and over" with considerable frequency in voice lessons and choral rehearsals. It is important to clearly define what is meant when this phrase is employed. Often, the phrase is mistaken for a specific vocal placement. In my opinion, its most valuable use is for alignment reinforcement. The phrase should be defined as another way of allowing the spine to lengthen as air is being used and, most importantly, to continually remind the choir to keep the A/O joint free. When properly released, the A/O and the correct alignment of the spine feels as if it is truly "up and over." It should be used exclusively to remind singers of free, balanced, and buoyant alignment.

Suggested Awareness Reminders

Verbal reinforcement on the part of the conductor is of crucial importance if alignment awareness is to be made part of the ensemble singers' rehearsal and performance life. Like it or not, choral conductors must understand that singers have found it extremely difficult to monitor both their singing and their bodies during a choral rehearsal. When surrounded by sound, singers often turn outward rather than inward to their own perceptions. Hence, their singing becomes external. A primary rehearsal rule should be to keep the choir in an awakened state both spiritually and mentally.

Use of Verbal Reminders to Reinforce Awareness

Constant verbal reminders concerning singers' awareness are of central importance in the rehearsal. In a private voice lesson, the voice teacher assumes the role of alignment monitor. As soon as a student becomes misaligned or unaware, the teacher perceives it and gives the appropriate correction. However, due to the group dynamic of the choral rehearsal, singers may lose touch with their bodies—that is, become perceptually unaware of their bodies, without correction. They become perceptually numb. It is important to develop an effective rehearsal technique that uses a variety of verbal cues that will reawaken their experience of themselves. Incorporate the phrases presented on the next page into your rehearsal language. Use the corresponding teaching card to take into rehearsal as a reminder, or write yourself a Post-It note to work these phrases into your instinctive rehearsal vocabulary.

The Use of Music and Folders in Rehearsal

There is a great deal of alignment sabotage that occurs in a choral rehearsal when choral octavos or choir folders are used. After remapping the core of the body, the use of music may destroy your work. When singers look at their music, they usually drag their necks forward, and the independence and mobility that was fostered in the A/O joint is destroyed. To avoid this, ask the choir to simply **tilt their heads to see the music.** Another remedy, if possible, is to use music stands in the rehearsal room.

Verbal Alignment Cues for Rehearsal

- Sing with your whole body, please.
- Are you keeping your heads independent and mobile?
- Are you thinking "up and over"?
- How is the joint of your head to your spine? Is it free? Can you sense it?
- Remember your weight-bearing spine, at your core.
- Are you balanced at your hip joints?
- Are your knees released and flexible?
- Are your feet feeling the floor?
- Are you feeling the tripod of your feet's arches?
- Are your heads dynamically poised?
- Are your backs free? Long and wide?
- Remember to organize around your spine, like an apple around a core.
- When you look at your music, just tilt your head. Don't drag your head forward.
- Remember to balance your arms. Don't pull them back or slump down.

Chapter 8

Spaciousness and Proper Vocal Production through the Use of the Sigh: Relaxation of the Vocal Tract—Creating Space

> I prefer tone quality to be varied. I must say that tone quality is more consistent among the great voices than among untrained and amateur voices. One of the problems in training voices is that since the world rewards singers on the size of the voice as well as on its beauty, or perhaps more on size than beauty, a lot of voices are forced beyond their physical capacity. Not everybody can be an Olympic Champion weightlifter. But most vocal studios, it seems to me, put their emphasis on developing a voice of size rather than on developing a voice of pitch integrity or quality. (p. 68)
>
> Robert Shaw
> *In Quest of Answers*

> Singing is like yawning. Many have misunderstood and tried to do both at the same time, hoping thereby to super induce the feeling of an "open throat." (p. 111)
>
> Giovanni Battista Lamperti
> *Vocal Wisdom*

The use of what is referred to as the "sigh" is one of the most valuable pedagogical tools available to choral conductors to determine the overall health of the vocal mechanism. Its power as a diagnostic tool should not be underestimated. A complete understanding of how to teach the proper technical execution of the sigh is at the core of all vocal instruction for a choir. Stated another way, if the choir cannot execute the sigh in a vocally correct way, then **all** consequent vocalism will suffer. Most importantly, a choral warm-up cannot and should not proceed until the sigh is correctly performed. The "recipe" for the correct performance of a vocal sigh is as follows:

Teaching Procedure for the Sigh

> ### Teaching Procedure for the Downward Sigh
> 1. Always sigh **downward** on "oo."
> 2. Create space through the use of "the cave."
> 3. Make certain the soft palate remains slightly raised throughout the sigh.
> 4. Teach and reinforce that the vocal sound remains **high** and **forward** as the sound descends in pitch.
> 5. Make certain the choir "wraps their lips around the sound."
> 6. Use a reinforcing physical gesture to ensure the above points are being successfully accomplished.

1. Always sigh downward on "oo."

The vowels "oo" and "ee" are the vowels that contain the most amount of head tone in all voices, but especially in women's and treble voices. To ensure the production of a good "oo" vowel, ask the choir to make certain the tongue is in a flat position in the mouth and to think that the tongue has a "pit" in it. Also make sure the lips are rounded and are truly participating in the production of the vowel. Asking the choir to imagine this shape tends to counterbalance any tongue tension the singers may bring to the vocalism from speech. Also make certain the vowel stays **high** and **forward.** Placing the heel of the hand on the forehead as one sighs can ensure this.

2. Create space by the use of the "cave."

Many of the vocal problems of amateur singers are created by their inability to create a proper spaciousness within the oral cavity. This ability is a central component to good vocal technique; in fact, it is the central building.

The steps for teaching the "cave" are as follows:

Finding the "Cave"

a. Have the choir feel for the fleshy cartilage at the front of their ear hole. Have them place a finger just forward of that point.

b. Once they have located that point, have the choir slowly drop their jaws until they feel an indentation or a "cave."

c. Ask the choir to create a small cave rather than a large one. A larger cave indicates a hyperextension of the jaw.

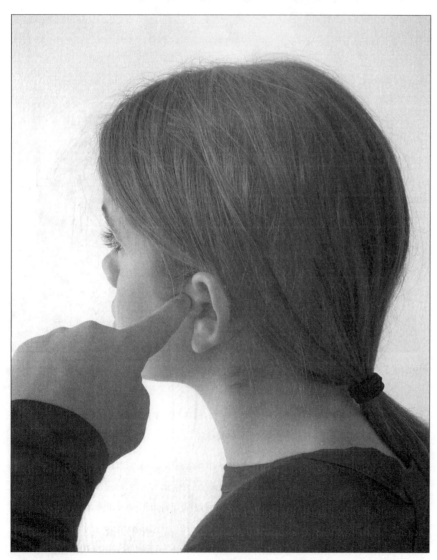

Figure 4 Locating the Cave

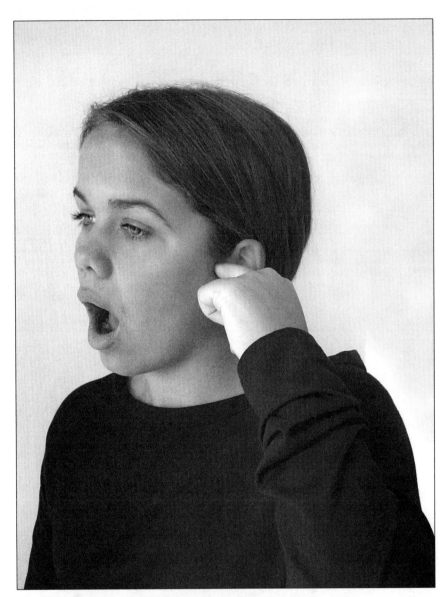

Figure 5 Dropping the Jaw Using the Cave

3. Make certain the soft palate remains slightly raised throughout the sigh.

Most inexperienced singers sing with a soft palate that is too low to direct vocal resonances into the masque or resonant bone structures in the face. The proper position is analogous to the position of the soft palate approximately one-quarter to one-half way through a yawn. Once in that position, the palate should remain in that raised position throughout the singing.

The raised palate throughout the singing process performs another very important technical aspect in the voice-building process: by remaining raised, register breaks are avoided, and a "mixing" of the vocal registers can be accomplished in a natural, healthy fashion.

4. Teach and reinforce that the vocal sound remains high and forward as the sound descends in pitch.

Another serious problem for inexperienced singers, especially in singers whose native tongue is American English, is that sounds tend to be produced too far back in the mouth. Hence, vocal sounds are dull and unresonant, which results in poor pitch (a flatness and dullness in the sound). The conductor must constantly reinforce the correct feeling of high and forward sound. The use of physical gesture is the most efficient way to accomplish this:

1. As the singers sigh downward on "oo," have them place the heel of their hand on their forehead. This gesture naturally ensures that the sound will be high and forward.

2. Have the singers perform the sigh without their hands on their foreheads.

3. Have the singers perform the sigh with their hands on their foreheads.

4. The conductor (and the choir) will hear a more brilliant and resonant sound!

5. Make certain the choir "wraps their lips around the sound."

Because of American English that is further influenced by regional dialects, vowel sounds tend to be resonentially spread and dull in sound. To counter this default tendency in singers, ask the singers to **wrap their lips around the sound.** This instruction accomplishes two important pedagogical objectives. First, by wrapping the lips around the sound, internal vertical spaciousness is maintained. Remember that this space was created by finding the cave and must be maintained. Second, you begin to teach vowel modification to the choir—that is, the ability to influence **both** the focus of the pitch and the color of the vowel by this participation of the lips in the vocal production process. It is important, however, for the choir to have the correct Body Map to know exactly what rounding is in this process. It is not their "lipstick lips" that create this, but rather the muscles that surround the mouth.

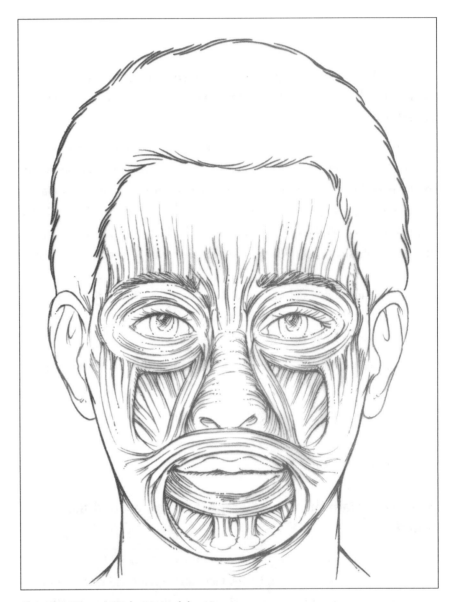

Figure 6 Correct Body Map of the Lips

6. Use a reinforcing physical gesture to ensure the above points are being successfully accomplished.

One of the problems in teaching a choral ensemble is certainly a type of vocal/technical accountability. In the private voice studio, this is easier to monitor and achieve because of the one-on-one nature of the instruction.

But in a choral situation, two problems are rampant. First, too many verbal instructions tend to get lost in the singers' ensemble unawareness until they are made habitual. Second, it is difficult for the conductor to ensure the singers are, in fact, doing what was asked of them.

Figure 7 Use of the Hand to Reinforce High and Forward Sound Placement

The way to accomplish vocal/technical accountability is through the use of physical gestures as a type of constant reinforcement for the singers until the correct singing sensations and awarenesses take over. Throughout this text, physical gestures will be suggested to reinforce many of the vocal principles being taught. The use of these gestures can bring a vibrant vocal accountability into an ensemble rehearsal and ensure that correct vocal technique will result. One should not underestimate either their power or their potency.

Another reason for using physical gestures is a simple pedagogical fact. After the conductor has verbally instructed the choir, such verbal instruction loses its potency with repetition until the choir has little or no response to the verbal explanation. This is a phenomenon of the group singing experience. To counter this, physical gestures provide an immediate kinesthetic link between technique, sound, and feeling—hence, its tremendous pedagogical power.

The "Up Over and Up" Gesture to Reinforce the Sigh

The gesture for reinforcing all aspects of the sigh is called the "up over and up" gesture, which can be demonstrated best with the following illustrations. After the initial explanations of the various components of the sigh, the gesture suggested here should **always** be used when the choir performs the sigh.

What You Should Hear When the Sigh Is Technically Correct

What should be the quality of the downward sigh that you hear in the choral sound? The sound should be light and airy. Remember that the primary objective of the sigh is to create space and to lower the vocal mechanism to a place where it can optimally function! The sound, which should be high and forward, manifests itself to the ear as a sound that is brilliant, colorful, and vibrant. Dullness and flatness of pitch are to be avoided. The vowel sound should be focused or "closed." If the lips are rounded (wrapping lips around the sound), the vowel will sound "focused," "narrow," and not "spread."

Figure 8 Beginning Position for "Up Over and Up" Sigh Gesture: START

Note that what you should hear is an important aspect of not only this particular technique, but of each of the techniques presented in this book. Your ability to diagnose **and** correct is directly related to what you can hear. This discriminating listening is an important part of the teaching process.

Figure 9 Second Hand Position in "Up Over and Up" Sigh Gesture Sequence: OVER

Figure 10 Third Hand Position in "Up Over and Up" Sigh Gesture Sequence: CONCLUDING UP

Sigh or Siren?

A strong distinction should be made between what has been described above as the "sigh" and the vocal technique most often called the "siren." Many conductors confuse the two or use either interchangeably. The **sigh** is always downward. It is a technique to allow singers to relax the larynx and establish spaciousness for singing. The **siren** (an upward glissando followed by a downward glissando) is sometimes used as a range extension exercise. As such, the siren is quite effective providing spaciousness is maintained throughout and sound is kept high and forward.

Despite its pedagogical gains, the siren is fraught with pedagogical problems. The most severe problem is that many amateur singers raise the larynx as they ascend and keep it in that position as they descend. Spaciousness is usually difficult to maintain. The laryngeal tension created by this exercise can only be reduced or eliminated through the use of the descending "sighs."

If sirens are used as a range extension exercise, **then therapeutic sighing to return the larynx to a relaxed position for singing should follow that exercise.** In no instance, however, should a siren be substituted in the mandatory part of the warm-up for a sigh. Sirens, if employed, should be used with great care. Remember to always restore spaciousness and a relaxed larynx after the use of a siren as a range extension exercise.

Chapter 9

Breathing: Inhalation and Exhalation

Finish the tone, but not the expiration. (p. 128)

Giovanni Battista Lamperti
Vocal Wisdom

In order for inhalation to be efficient (avoiding maladjustment of any part of the vocal tract), it must be silent.

Tension is not "support." Increased muscle resistance is not necessarily an indication of better breath management.

"Relaxation is a relative term; breathing involves muscle antagonism (and synergism) just as does any other physical activity. Energy for the singing voice demands muscle coordination between the breath source (the motor) and the larynx (the vibrator). (p. 39)

Richard Miller
The Structure of Singing

In considering teaching techniques for instruction in the breathing process, many of us overlook the obvious. We assume that choirs instinctively inhalate and exhalate because they do so to live. However, inhalation and exhalation for singing require different awarenesses, which can only be achieved through the use of Body Mapping. To deliver the most effective instruction to the choir, two resources should be used.

First, every choir member should have in their choir folder a copy of the booklet *The Structures and Movement of Breathing* by Barbara Conable (GIA). Beginning on page 15 of that booklet, the choir should read a page a day concerning the breathing process and view the anatomical drawings contained therein.

Second, the core instruction for inhalation and exhalation must be taken from the content of the video *Evoking Sound: Body Mapping Principles and Basic Conducting Technique* (GIA). To correctly have the singers map the mechanisms of inhalation and exhalation, conductors should either **show** the breathing portion of the video or be able to comfortably **demonstrate** the eight-handed breathing demonstration exactly as it occurs on the video. To ensure conductors learn this material, it is not replicated here; you must watch the visual presentation on the video because it is insufficient to describe it in words.

Inhalation: Remapping the Trachea

An important Body Mapping point concerning inhalation should be covered prior to teaching eight-handed breathing. Many choirs breathe and use breath improperly because they do not inhale correctly. They unknowingly use muscles for swallowing to take air into the body. This seems to be the default mechanism in most singers, and the corresponding Body Map must be corrected if breathing is to improve.

1. Ask the choir, "What is the anatomical make-up of your throat?" The answers will astound you. The proper response should be that there are two "pipes" in the neck.

2. Ask the choir to label those "pipes." They should respond with "trachea" and "esophagus."

3. Ask the choir which tube is "in the front." Many will respond with an incorrect Body Map, saying that the esophagus is in the front. That is because the esophagus is the tube for which they are most aware because it is used for swallowing and ingestion. However, air is taken into the lungs through the front tube (the trachea). Many perceive the esophagus as being the front tube. If that is their Body Map, then they will never breathe correctly.

Air is taken in through the trachea, the front tube. An aural sign of an incorrect Body Map is that breath tends to be noisy, even raspy. When air is taken through the front tracheal tube, breath is **quiet.** An additional by-product of this remapping is that air taken into the body in such a way will encourage a lower larynx.

It has been my experience that no single factor affects the quality of choral sound more than alignment. Poor alignment tends to grow insidiously within the choral rehearsal if the conductor does not keep it in check. While the principles presented above appear to be rather simple, they are pedagogically potent. Without accurate Body Maps and sensory awareness, it is difficult (if not impossible) to obtain a truly outstanding choral sound.

If one uses these principles, choral tone will achieve a new vibrancy and resonance heretofore unheard within the ensemble. However, both conductors and singers must realize that this work needs to be done in every warm-up and reinforced throughout the rehearsal. The conductor must become vigilant and be an advocate for alignment, without which the ensemble will labor unnecessarily to sing.

There is a saying among teachers that what is usually easiest learned is hardest taught. Alignment principles are easily acquired, but they require constant vigilance by the conductor.

Suffice it to say that my use of these materials and reinforcement of the concepts presented has vastly improved the singing of choirs I conduct. As was stated in the "Alignment and Body Awareness" portion of this book, a repertoire of verbal reminders is central to the pedagogical reinforcement process. With these materials as the core of your instruction, the following phrases can be used in rehearsal to reinforce the singers' Body Maps for inhalation and exhalation. These cues are reprinted on the teaching cards available separately from this volume from the publisher (GIA, G-6397I). Use the cards in your rehearsal, or write the phrases below on Post-It notes to take into rehearsal as reminders.

Verbal Cues for Inhalation and Exhalation

- Are you aware of your breathing?
- Breathing moves from the top down, not like a glass filling up.
- Remember that breathing moves into the body in a wavelike motion, from top to bottom.
- Breathe through your front tube (trachea), not the back tube (esophagus).

- Breathe without using your swallowing muscles.
- When you breathe, your ribs do not expand; they make outward and inward excursions.
- You breathe at breathing joints, and those breathing joints are in the back.
- When you take air in, your spine gathers, like a cat preparing to pounce.
- When you are using air to sing, your spine lengthens, like a cat pouncing.
- Remember what space your lungs occupy in your chest cavity.
- Your diaphragm works on inhalation. Leave the area alone to dome back up on exhalation.
- Experience the whole cylinder of your abdominal wall.
- Outward and downward release allow your spine to lengthen.
- As you sustain the phrase, is your spine lengthening?

Breathing: Teaching "Support" or "On the Breath" Singing

Once the inhalation and exhalation process has been remapped with the use of the eight-handed breathing method (on the *Evoking Sound* video), the concept of support can be introduced. A synonym for this is the phrase "singing on the breath." Technically, singing on the breath is the process by which breath, movement of air, and phonation are all interconnected into one body sensation. It is the feeling of those interconnected activities that must be initially experienced and **not** explained as separate component parts.

It has been my experience that after remapping the inhalation and exhalation process, it is most efficient to have the choir experience support. Support is a complex interaction of breath and phonation that is complicated to explain to the novice choral singer. It is most efficiently taught through a singular exercise, which I have found to be both quick and efficient. This exercise has been described by some as the **Breath "Kneading" Exercise.**

Steps in Teaching the Breath "Kneading" Exercise

1. Select a simple exercise, preferably one with upward leaps, such as the vocalise contained in this book that is do–so, do–so, do–re–mi–re–do.

2. Ask singers to put their left hand in an open, flat position at navel level. This subconsciously locates the depth of the breath necessary in a "supported" breath.

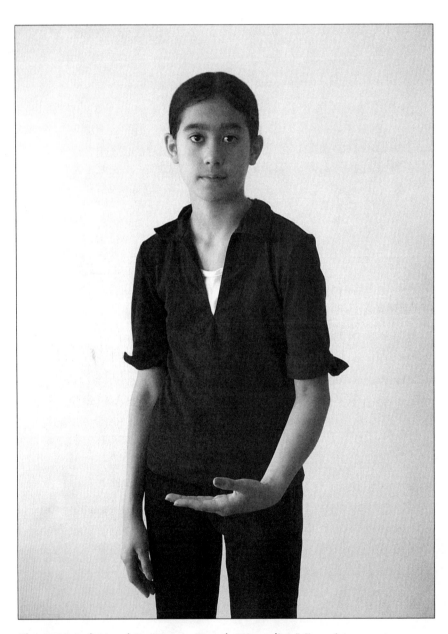

Figure 11 Left-Hand Position in Breath "Kneading" Exercise

3. Instruct the singers on the circular forward motion of the right hand. Note that the hand should be held in a fist, with thumb facing forward. The fist gently contacts the left hand at the bottom of the circle. Also make note of the size of the circle made by the right hand. The speed of the right hand is the tempo of the exercise. Note that the movement of the right hand also represents physically the constant movement of air in the singing process.

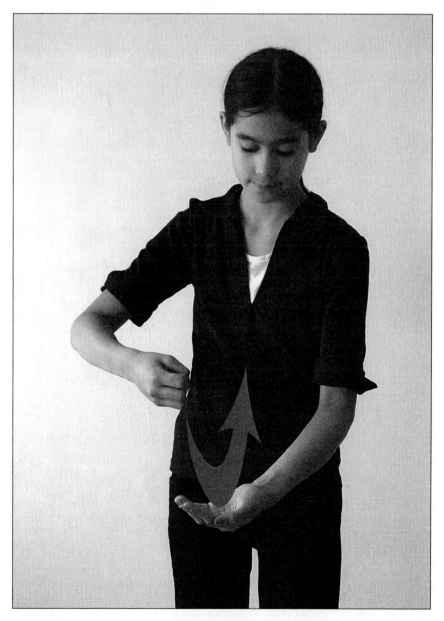

Figure 12 Right-Hand Movement in Breath "Kneading" Exercise

Figure 13 Right-Hand Sequential Circular Movement in Breath "Kneading" Exercise – Front View

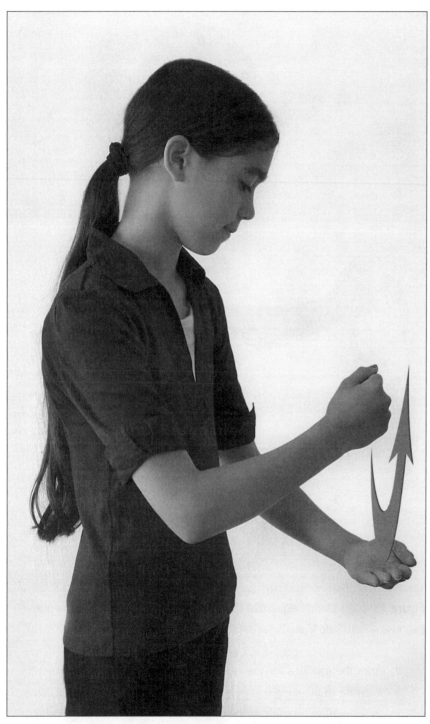

Figure 14 Right-Hand Sequential Circular Movement in Breath "Kneading" Exercise – Right Side View

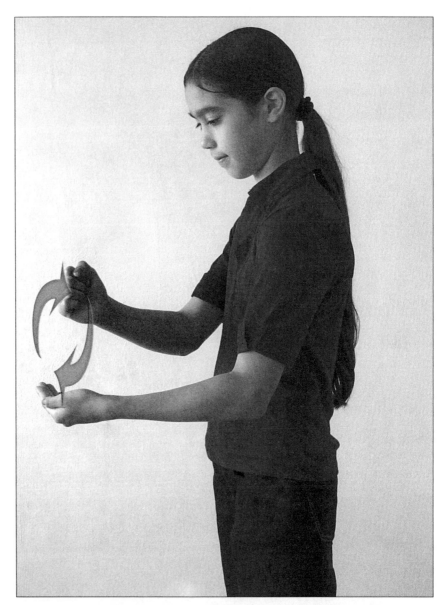

Figure 15 Right-Hand Sequential Circular Movement in Breath "Kneading" Exercise – Left Side View

4. After the motions for the exercise have been learned, connect the exercise to the sung vocalise suggested above. Perform the exercise in sequential repetition, moving up a half step each time, with a breath between each exercise. **Be certain the circular motion of the right hand never stops or slows throughout the performance of these exercises.** Use the notated accompaniment in this book for this exercise. Tell the choir that the sensation they feel while

performing this exercise is "support" or "on the breath" singing. It is important to label this sensation in the singers.

5. After the choir performs the exercise correctly with physical gesture as detailed above, it is important to have the singers experience "off the breath" singing. Learning occurs when the choir is able to distinguish when something is not something else! To do this, have the choir simply raise the level of their hand to upper chest or neck level and perform the exercise again. The very different sound should be labeled immediately as an "off the breath" sound, which is undesirable in singing.

Figure 16 Right-Hand High Sequential Circular Movement in Breath "Kneading" Exercise (to teach sensation of "off the breath" singing)

Use of Breath "Kneading" Exercise to Document Connection to Singing

Aside from the pedagogical benefits of the breath kneading exercise, this exercise performs a valuable extra function for the choral conductor. I don't think there would be any disagreement among voice teachers or choral conductors that aside from basic vocal technique, physical and spiritual energy are important and indispensable components for an alive and vital vocal sound. While aspects of vocal technique are a challenge to teach to any choir, the aspects of "energy" and "spiritual energy" are, perhaps, even more elusive.

If you look at the pictures above concerning the proper execution of this exercise, you will notice the size of the circular movement of the hands. The speed of the movement of the hands is determined by the tempo you are about to sing. Size and energy of that circular gesture are philosophically important. If the size of the gesture is correct, then its energy will be correct. However, in most cases, choir members will respond with a gesture that is small and lacking energy. This is a reflection of their spirit at the moment. It may also be a reflection of their personality or spiritual demeanor. Persons who are quiet, afraid, timid, self-doubting, or noncommittal will most likely do this exercise with a small, unenergetic gesture. While your goal should not be to "change the person," you can maximize the energy brought to singing and also cause the person to "open up" through the encouragement of a large circle (as shown previously in the photos).

Only begin singing the vocalise when the gesture is of the right size and the right energy. Encourage your singers by your modeling of the correct breath kneading gesture.

A word of caution: Some choir members might be unable to do this! It is important to understand why. If any of your singers have difficulties in life (e.g., illness, personal issues, etc.), they will not be able to make the large circular motion you are requesting. This is because something in life is closing them and they have formed a protective wall around themselves. You should not address those issues in any way; rather, continue to try to draw these singers out through the encouragement of the gesture. Focus on the gesture, not on any issue. Perhaps through this approach, you can help them open up and trust themselves within the environment of the choir.

The Pros and Cons of Diaphragm Activity

In some of my earlier writings, the words "diaphragm activity" were used to describe a specific technique that was connected to enhancing diction. Experience and time has shown that this term is confusing and, in all likelihood, creates more problems than it solves. The danger in using the term is that inexperienced singers believe that diaphragm activity **is** support. Warm-up activities that use repeated sibilant consonants, such as "f–f–f–f–f–f," "sh–sh–sh–sh–sh–sh," etc., may be valuable if their objective is correct articulation of consonants. However, used as a "breath exercise" or confused as a support exercise, the use of such exercises can be detrimental. Aside from the kinesthetic of feeling the breath in the body "too high," these exercises can also cause the following problems:

- The sensation of repeated sibilants without sung sound is not the sensation one feels when air is released from the body through the vocal chords and transformed into vocal sound.
- The constant release of air tends to dry the vocal chords, possibly leading to vocal problems.
- The repeated use of sibilated consonants causes the larynx to raise into a higher position and, thus, works in opposition to principles presented earlier for healthy vocal singing.
- The repeated use of such sibilants can also produce jaw, tongue, and lip tension.

Lip Trill Dangers

Lip trills can be valuable vocal training devices when used under the supervision of a studio teacher. Many choral conductors employ them as part of their choral warm-up as a technique to teach support, and at times to awaken singing resonances. However, lip trills employed in a choral situation could create conceptual confusion and actually lead to poor vocalism.

While lip trills certainly engage the breath mechanism and move the breath in an ongoing way, the danger lies in the fact that the kinesthetic sensation of lip trills has little connection to the actual sensation of supported singing. Moreover, the feeling of how sound is produced with a lip trill is not the same feeling as singing. Air in a lip trill is expelled and used in a highly inefficient manner. The lip buzzing involved with a lip trill also tends to create a great amount of jaw, tongue, and lip tension for the singers. Lip trills also tend to raise the larynx into a position that is too high for free, relaxed singing. It is probably in the best interest of the choir to avoid lip trills as a part of their ensemble warm-up diet.

Chapter 10
Building Resonance

Each singer has a different physiognomy and, therefore, a slightly different sense of focus. This precludes a teacher being able to direct a tone to a specific place such as "behind the front teeth," "in the nose," and "in the sinuses." As a student achieves a certain amount of vocal freedom and coordination of the various parts of the vocal mechanism, as well as a good mental concept of the sound he should be making, proper focus will result. (p. 96)

Richard Miller
The Structure of Singing

Creating General Resonances

Of all the steps in the warm-up process, this is the one that is either most often missed or performed at the wrong point in the pedagogical sequence. The author has found that if this "step" is not taught and achieved at its appropriate point in the warm-up process, then the vocalism for the rest of the rehearsal becomes unruly and, at times, unusable. If this step is omitted, irreversible vocal damage is created for the rest of that particular rehearsal.

Instead of correcting, many conductors attribute this to a "bad day." Initial generation of resonance through activation of the resonators creates the raw materials for **all** vocalism that is to follow. At this stage of the warm-up, it is important to understand the pedagogical imperative contained in initial resonance vocalizes. So important is this step that it can never be missed, and it must **always** occur at this point in the warm-up, **after** inhalation and exhalation and **before** any phonation takes place in the rehearsal.

Another important point to remember is that if this step is omitted, singers will begin singing with the resonances they have used in their speaking voices all day. Not only are those resonances insufficient sound "fuel" for the singing process, but there needs to be a resonential transition between speaking and singing. In vocal terms, the conductor must be assured that sufficient head resonances have been generated to be "focused" and directed for appropriate tone color later in the warm-up process.

In each warm-up, correct and healthy singing resonances and the physical "homes" or "apartments" of those resonances must be "awakened" and "activated." The most efficient route to those resonances is through humming and chewing exercises. The teaching techniques for these exercises are as follows:

Humming and Chewing: Resonance-Generating Exercises

1. Begin the exercise by asking the choir to "hum and chew" in their middle register on the consonants "MMMM."
2. Make certain the choir hums and chews with teeth apart and lips lightly together.
3. Make certain the hum and chew is spacious. Ask singers to check their "caves" (see "Teaching Procedure for the Sigh").
4. Make certain the humming and chewing is high and forward. To ensure this is being done and the sound does not rest in the jowls, ask the choir to place the heel of their hand on their forehead as they hum and chew.
5. To make certain resonances are generated in all registers of the voice, ask the singers to hum and chew also in their upper register and their lower register.
6. To ensure there is enough head tone in the sound, it is often helpful to immediately follow each humming and chewing exercise with a downward sigh on "oo" and the appropriate supporting hand gesture (see "Spaciousness and Proper Vocal Production through the Use of the Sigh: Relaxation of the Vocal Tracts—Creating Space").

Specific Resonances

After a general resonance has been created through humming and chewing via the use of voiced consonants, it is then the task of the warm-up to further refine that resonance into an appropriate sound—or rather, the color that is needed to rehearse the pieces for the day. There is a basic decision to be made by the conductor at this point in the warm-up process: Is a "bright" sound needed or is a "dark" sound needed? This is dependent upon the literature to be rehearsed. I have found that the terms "bright" and "dark" are somewhat dangerous to employ in a choral rehearsal because of the inconsistency of the meaning of those words when translated in singers' minds. How "bright or how "dark" should a sound be? It is all relative to one's perception. Overly bright sounds may translate into sounds produced with a high larynx or excessively high palate. Sounds that are too dark may be the result of a "jowel" placement that is too far back, or from a tension-ridden tongue. Both extremes must be avoided.

I have found two approaches that are effective in further focusing general resonances. One approach would be to ask the choir to either imagine a **tall/narrow vowel** or a **round vowel.** In the warm-up, you **must** make a choice. If you do not, the choir will usually default to the vowel shape that is most closely associated with their speaking dialect! By simply asking the choir to visualize the shape of the vowel, the appropriate resonances will be generated. Also by using this approach, you have begun to teach diction through appropriate vowel color.

The second approach is to affect vowel color through breath. For a "brighter" vowel color, ask the choir to take a "cool breath." For a darker vowel color, ask the choir to take a "warm breath." For the darker vowel colors, it may be helpful to once again ask the choir to place the heel of their hand on their forehead to ensure high and forward placement.

After the conductor has decided the pedagogical route, then the singing of vocalizes can begin. For that purpose, consult the **Core Vocal Exercises** presented later in this book.

Developing Specific Resonances

1. Ask the choir to sing either tall, narrow vowels or round vowels.
2. Ask the choir to take either a cool breath (brighter resonances) or a warm breath (darker resonances).
3. Begin vocalizing on the vowels "oo" and "ee" only!

The Pedagogical Necessity of Head Tone

If one were to ask what the single most important ingredient for the building of a healthy vocal sound is, the answer most certainly would be pedagogical insistence upon head tone. In women's and treble voices, there is a large resonential capability for the use of head tone. Male voices have head tone, but not in the same large quantities that are possessed by women's and treble voices. Without sufficient head tone, it is almost impossible to have a wide range of dynamics, and it is next to impossible to have crescendos or decrescendos. It is also difficult to vary tone color for different musical styles because the coloring device for changing color (head tone) is absent. Finally, without sufficient head tone in the sound, serious pitch problems will abound. Further, if voices are not developed with a "top-downward" mentality (i.e., bringing head tone downward into the voice), then register breaks are developed and nourished in the voice. Careful selection of vowels for vocalizing is directly related to head tone development. "Oo" and "ee" are often referred to as "head tone vowels." Of all the vowels in English, they are the two vowels that are most abundant in their capacity for carrying head tone. In essence, all vowel colors, in my opinion, should grow from a correct production of "oo" and "ee." **No other vowels should be used at the beginning of the warm-up process for inexperienced choirs.**

Choosing the Sequence of Exercises: Begin with Middling the Voice

The actual singing part of the warm-up must proceed with an equal diet of exercises that use all registers of the voice. For beginning choirs, it is always desirable to use exercises that descend rather than ascend. The overall objective of any warm-up should be to bring as much head tone into the vocal sound.

Next, exercises that begin in the middle registers of the voice are best to use at the beginning of the warm-up. These should be employed to ensure engagement of the support apparatus to the sounds being performed without the threat of excessive range requirements. The recommended starting key for all warm-ups of this type is E-flat.

After singing one or two warm-up exercises in the middle register, then proceed to exercises that explore and build approaches to other registers of the voice, high and low. Those exercises should begin in range-appropriate keys. However, it is important to note that one should not proceed from these "middling" exercises until the vocal sound is on the breath and there is sufficient connected vocalic flow and musical line.

The Logic of Vowel Closure and Proper Use of the Lips in Closing Vowel Sounds

One of the most important concepts in the choral warm-up is the pedagogical understanding surrounding the building of vowel **color.** In my opinion, it is one of the most effective tools for not only the immediate improvement of choral sound, but also long-term vocal health of the choir.

In a later section of this text, a detailed procedure for teaching diction will be discussed (see "Six-Step Diction Teaching Technique"). Always remember that because vowels and consonants are used in the warm-up, the foundations of good diction are built in the warm-up. Consequently, decisions concerning vowel color must be made in the early stages of a choir's pedagogical life. Moreover, these are more than just pedagogical decisions. They are decisions concerning the philosophy of building choral sound.

If one begins with the viewpoint that inexperienced singers will bring their speaking dialect into the rehearsal and apply it to their singing, then it logically follows that there must be a strong pedagogical distinction made in the singers' mind on the differences between sung language and spoken language. In American English, vowel sounds can be generally characterized as "too wide," "spread," and "open." That means either the lip embouchure either is too wide and open **or** the lips do not participate in the singing process. Both are dangerous and will destroy choral ensemble sound.

One cardinal rule must always be in place, regardless of one's own vowel "preferences." The internal, vertical spaciousness of the vowel must always be present. The conductor must always guard against the loss of internal spaciousness when discussing lip position with the choir. To lose any degree of internal spaciousness will destroy healthy, vibrant choral sounds!

With that being said, the most important pedagogical tool available that directly influences choral sound is vowel color—or rather, vowel shape. The lips are the major arbiters in the production of this color. "Wrap your lips around the sound" is the phrase that I have found most efficient in a choral rehearsal. The use of this phrase implies to the singers that their lips surround something. That something is the vertical internal spaciousness of the vowel as taught throughout this approach, beginning with the sigh. Wrapping your lips around the sound closes the vowel. Closing the vowel, to my way of thinking, progresses through a series of vocal colors, from overtone rich to more focused overtones. Closing the vowels also allows for one to more efficiently get to both the core of the pitch and the core of the vocal sound, or its acoustic fundamental. It also seems logical, then, that the following rule must be observed: the larger the choir, the more vowels must be closed. This has a parallel in the instrumental world. When I was a clarinetist, I played in wind ensembles where all the clarinetists used the same mouthpieces and reeds. This was an attempt by the conductor to ensure a more uniform overtone series throughout the ensemble. Orchestras sometimes dictate specific vintage instruments within string sections for similar reasons. The vehicle for choral ensemble acoustic similarity is the amount of vowel closure that is asked of the choir. The text presented later on teaching diction will discuss the role vowel closure (or lack thereof) plays in the musical style of a choral ensemble (see "Teaching Diction through the Choral Warm-Up").

Vowel closure and the amount the conductor asks for is a product of one's personal choral experience combined with one's choral listening experience and color sense. Just as an artist faces decisions each day as to which colors to select from an entire world of color, the choral conductor must likewise select from his or her aural palate of vowel colors. Those colors can only be achieved through vowel shape and vowel closure.

A word must be added here concerning experienced, trained singers within any choral ensemble. Vowels employed in the studio and on stage that are beautiful in those situations are probably too "open" for a choral situation. I have heard so many beautiful voices compromised in choral rehearsals because the conductor keeps "shooshing" the voice or telling the singer to sing "quieter." However, that is not the issue. It is a question of vowel! That singer's beautiful color is needed in the ensemble, so that singer should never compromise vocal technique to "blend." The singer should instead simply close vowel sounds more than he or she does in the studio or on stage. Singers who share both the choral experience and the stage experience must use the vowel as their primary tool in adapting to the specific performance needs of both.

There is another reason vowel "closure" is important. By asking the singers to "wrap their lips around the sound," the "oo" vowels mix into the choral sound. The "oo" vowel is often referred to as the "helper" vowel in that it is a "head tone" vowel. By modifying the vowel toward "oo," you are infusing the healthy qualities of "oo" into choral sound. Decisions concerning vowel closure are a necessary part of building sound in the choral ensemble and must be constantly made during the warm-up process. Further, conductors must be constantly vigilant in listening for vowel color as they lead the choir through the warm-up and rehearsal.

Remapping the Lips

One of the difficulties in referring to the lips is that most, if not all, singers have their lips improperly mapped! Singers must accurately map the musculature that surrounds the lips. Many criticisms made by voice teachers about choral conductors relate to undoing lip tension created via the choral rehearsal, which is the result of inaccurate Body Maps. The choir should be shown the diagram below, or view both diagrams on pages 21 and 22 of *The Structures and Movement of Breathing* by Barbara Conable (GIA). Once correctly mapped and reinforced in subsequent rehearsals, the lips will be used correctly to assist with vowel closure.

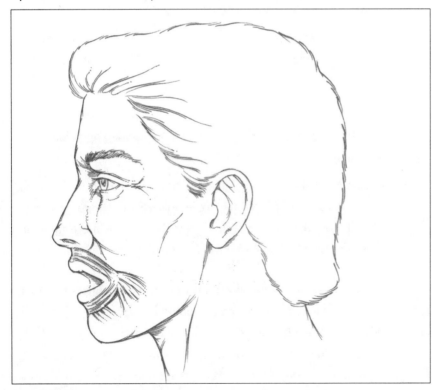

Figure 17 Anatomy of the Lips

Listening for Musical Line and Vocalic Flow

Of all the listening skills that are important for any conductor, listening skills that have to do with specific aspects of vocal technique are central to the pedagogical growth of any choir. Aside from the ability to teach specific vocal technique to the choir, the ability to hear that vocal technique correctly employed via the sound the conductor hears during the rehearsal process is most important. As the conductor hears the sound of the choir, there must be an immediate and spontaneous action/reaction to the sound. Pedagogical corrections, if necessary, must follow. The difficulty, though, is how the conductor can train himself or herself to hear these vocal technique issues.

Inherent in the best listening skill is the ability to hear vocalic flow—or the sound qualities of the vowel and its inherent aural forward motion. The conductor must search for the following every second of the rehearsal process:

1. Does the vowel (forward motion of the breath) move forward at all times? (Note: By the strictest of definitions, this should be considered the most basic definition of "musical line.")

2. Does the vowel have a definitive color? In other words, is there an aural representation of the vowel as being either tall and narrow (bright sound) or round (darker sound).

3. Does the vowel move forward constantly and with freedom and energy?

4. Is the forward-moving vowel produced without laryngeal pressure or tension?

5. As the singers sing a musical line, do they **follow** their own vowels? That is, does it seem that each vowel follows the other incessantly and without break, and that those vowels spin outward from their faces, almost seemingly in front of them?

One of the difficulties in learning to hear musical line is that one simply has not taken the time to listen to literally hundreds of examples of musical line on recording. If one has heard enough examples of beautiful musical line, then one would come to establish in one's own ear the "aural model" for expressive musical line. Recordings of great singers, oboists, and string quartets should form the basic choral library of all conductors.

Life Issues with Musical Line

It cannot be argued that musical line is certainly the result of proper vocal technique that focuses upon the correct use of air. However, an equal partner in the creation of musical line is human energy provided by the individual. The most compelling musical line is that which is connected in the most intimate way to one's life and one's spiritual core. Central to one's spiritual beliefs is one's commitment to those spiritual issues. Musical line will never be aurally recognizable unless there is a commitment to life issues on the part of the singer **and** the conductor.

The ability to move sound forward is also an issue of trust and belief in oneself. That trust creates an internal energy and life force that is infectious to all who come in contact with it. Without that force, it is difficult, if not impossible, to engage one's body to "support" the forward movement of air. The removal and identification of those barriers is as much a part of the singing process as is vocal technique. Constant education and discussion is necessary. However, before that can take place, the conductor must be philosophically clear as to his or her understanding of those issues. *The Musician's Spirit* (GIA, 2002) addresses at length the use of story in the rehearsal to explore these themes.

Absence of Love: Normal Illusion

Aside from all the factors concerning musical line, there is an important factor that can never be ignored. Honest musical line cannot exist unless there is love and care present in the rehearsal room and performance space at all times. I have known many conductors, several very famous, who believe their ensembles sing with incredible musical line. On close listening, they move sound forward by sheer force of their will and personality. Musical sound is not transported but rather physically propelled. The reason these conductors believe their ensembles have musical line is because of what psychology calls "normal illusion."

According to psychologists, normal illusion is when you hear, in essence, what you believe you hear regardless of what is really going on. Does the choir sound musical? Yes, on a very surface level. But if one listens for truly human elements, the soundscape of the vocalic flow of the musical line is barren and devoid of rhythmic spontaneity that can only be borne out of love and care. It is impossible for musical line to contain this ingredient of "life honesty" unless the conductor understands the essences of love and compassion and practices them as a part of his or her life...period. I know conductors who profess to be masters of essence of human connection when they themselves are inhumane to all those around them. Love and loving in life cannot be interrupted or imagined. It must be lived, daily and constantly. When such a quality exists in life, then it will exist in the music. Perhaps the quote below best summarizes this "human component" for musical line.

> So Socrates was mistaken: it's not the unexamined life that is not worth living; it's the uncommitted life. There is no smaller package in the world than that of a person all wrapped up in himself. Love is our business. (p. 12)

William Sloane Coffin
The Heart Is a Little to the Left

Vowel Development Hierarchy

Many pedagogical choices are certainly left up to the conductor's discretion. One of the most important choices concerns what vowels to choose for vocalizing the choir. The choice of vowel, or rather one's "vowel philosophy," should form the pedagogical core of the vocal development of the choir. The choice of vowel selection should be one of the most contemplated decisions a conductor makes in the process of constructing the choral warm-up.

Many will argue that you should use all the vowels to create a "balanced vowel diet" for the choir. Well, this sounds great, but it does not work efficiently. Rather, view the building of sound in a choral ensemble through a logical process of vowel production that emphasizes both the sonic qualities of the vowel and its mechanical production.

If one's philosophy is to bring as much head tone into the choral sound as is possible at all times for healthy vocal production, then it follows logically that one should begin vocalizing the choir on the vowels that contain the largest "quantity" of head tone: the pure vowels "oo" and "ee," and the mixed vowel sound as is demonstrated by the German umlauted "u" (ü). Other vowels should then be introduced using those vowels as springboards.

That is, "ah" should only be introduced by either "oo" or "ee." Similarly, "eh" should be introduced when preceded by "oo" and "ee." Hence, all the exercises in this volume use primarily "oo" and "ee." Consonants are then selected to reflect articulation style.

When introducing vowel sounds to the choir, it is also important to teach the mechanics of vowel production. The approximate positioning of the tongue and lips must be taught and constantly reinforced by the conductor. The basic formulae for "oo" and "ee" are as follows:

Teaching the "oo" Vowel

1. The tongue must lie flat in the mouth, with the tip of the tongue resting lightly behind the front teeth.
2. To avoid a "humping" or thickening of the tongue, the choir should imagine that they have a "pit" in their tongue.
3. The vowel should feel as if it is moving outward, high and forward through the cheekbones.
4. The heel of the hand should be placed on the forehead to reinforce high and forward placement.
5. The lips should look like "oo." They should be slightly rounded without tension.
6. The larynx must remain in a relaxed position.

Teaching the "ee" Vowel

1. The tongue position is high for this vowel.
2. The tip of the tongue is anchored against the lower front teeth.
3. The vowel should feel as if it is moving outward, high and forward through the cheekbones.
4. The heel of the hand should be placed on the forehead to reinforce high and forward placement.
5. The lips should be slightly rounded to promote focus in the vowel.

Consonants in Vocalization

Many conductors choose consonants for vocalization without much thought as to their pedagogical imperative. Consonants can both build and reinforce the correct production of a sound, or they can be a detrimental force in the production of a sound. One must choose consonants for vocalization with great care. There is a hierarchical order for consonants; some consonants should be first choices, second choices, and some should seldom, if ever, be used.

Note for all consonants: Make certain the consonants are always articulated quickly and do not carry undue weight into the following vowel. Undue weight on the consonant will cause pitch problems and inhibit musical line.

First Line Consonants: D–N–V

These consonants should be the first choice for vocalization, especially with inexperienced choirs. Use these consonants at the beginning of the warm-up, regardless of the experience of the singers.

D   This consonant is one of the most valuable for vocalization because it allows for both efficient use of support and, when correctly articulated, a natural high and forward placement of the choral sound. More than any other, this consonant encourages singers to stay on the breath. It is useful in building healthy marcato articulation that is connected to the breath. Remember, however, to reinforce the correct articulation of the consonant "D." When correctly articulated, the consonant is formed with the tongue **pointed** toward the ridge above the upper teeth.

N   This consonant is most useful for building legato. Because it is a voiced consonant, be certain it carries pitch when used. This will encourage both proper support and accurate pitch. The use of this consonant naturally encourages a high, forward sound.

V   The "V" consonant is valuable for building resonances that are high and forward. It is also helpful to teach economical and measured use of the air stream.

Second Line Consonants: T–M

T   This consonant is useful when more detached articulations are desired or more rhythmic clarity is required. The problem with this consonant is that while it tends to clarify rhythm, the production of the consonant itself releases air that could otherwise be spent on the vowel. Repeated use of this consonant also makes it difficult to keep vocal sound on the breath and supported.

M   The "M" consonant is another useful consonant for building legato. However, when used, two safeguards must be in place. First, make certain the singers have lips lightly together and teeth slightly apart. This consonant is problematic because singers bring undue tension to its production with lip tension and clenched teeth.

Second, because of the tendency of English-speaking choirs, this consonant will naturally produce a "jowel vowel"—that is, a vowel that has a backward placement and is not high and forward. Physical gesture (i.e., heel of hand on forehead) is often effective in maintaining proper placement of this consonant. Like "N," this consonant is also a voiced consonant and carries pitch. Make certain all "M" consonants in vocalization are pitched.

Slenderizing Consonant: P

P   This consonant is extremely useful when the choral texture is too "heavy" and the sound is so "thick" that it has trouble moving forward. Have the choir vocalize on the consonant "P" followed with a vowel of your choice. Then rehearse the literature using this neutral syllable to lighten the choral texture.

Consonants to Never Use: L–Y–R

While there may be situations where it is justified, these consonants usually create more problems in choral situations than they cure. Thus, they should be avoided.

L   This consonant is used by many choral directors in vocalizing. For American choirs, it is a dangerous consonant. The only correct articulation of the consonant "L" is to sing it "tip of the tongue." If the consonant is not correctly articulated, the vowels are that follow are usually placed back in the throat and the sound becomes unfocused and somewhat swallowed.

Y   This consonant is extremely dangerous. Many choral directors use this consonant to promote jaw relaxation. While this may be accomplished, one must be vigilant that the sound does not lose high and forward placement.

R   The consonant "R" should be avoided for vocalization because of the difficulty of maintaining a high and forward placement. The American reflexive "R" should be avoided.

Chapter 11
Vocal Technique "Recipes"

One should never sing a note totally forte or totally piano. Pablo Casals said that one never plays just *forte* or piano; one plays within a *forte* or within a *piano*. If one observes this principle, each note then becomes an event unto itself, regardless of its temporal value.

Robert Shaw
Rehearsal with the Westminster Symphonic Choir
(November 1991)

All dynamic levels are relative to the size of the instrument that is producing them. To request the large dramatic instrument, as we have seen, to sing as soft a *pianissimo* in actual amplitude as can the *leggiero* instrument is as nonsensical as to require the *leggiero* to match the *fortissimo* of the dramatic voiced. An unwillingness to realize this proportional relationship of dynamic level within each instrument is partly the reason why falsetto and finta practices have increasingly crept into the vocal pedagogy of the past decade or so. A trumpet is not expected to produce the *piano* dynamic level of a recorder. (p. 180)

Richard Miller
The Structure of Singing

Dynamics

To build dynamics within a choir, the first prerequisite is to have sufficient head tone contained in the sound. Without head tone, there will be little, if any, dynamic range possible. The most important principle to teach the choir is that the feeling of a fully supported *forte* sound is the same body feeling as singing a *piano* dynamic. Consequently, the best way to teach variations in dynamics is to teach *forte* and *piano* adjacently so the extremes of the dynamic range can be produced with the same supported, energetic body and support system. The steps for teaching dynamics are as follows:

> ### Teaching Dynamics
>
> 1. Sing an exercise that uses a repeated *forte* sound, such as "Doo–Doh–Dah–Deh–Dee." Make certain all vowels are **spacious, high,** and **forward.**
> 2. Immediately repeat the same vowel sequence, but this time at a *piano* dynamic. Maintain the space of the vowel!
> 3. To achieve a colorful *piano* dynamic, make certain the space of the *forte* vowel is maintained. Achieve the *piano* dynamic by simply "closing" the vowel. That is, bring "the lips around the sound." For a more *piano* sound, increase the closure of the vowel.
> 4. Remember that closing the vowel does **not** mean closing the internal space. It refers only to the use of the lips to focus and color the vowel.

Crescendo/Decrescendo

The ability to perform artistic crescendos and decrescendos is one of the more challenging vocal techniques for the choral conductor. If left pedagogically unattended, improper crescendos and decrescendos can destroy healthy choral singing. The reason for this is that central to the execution of the crescendo/decrescendo are head tone, proper vowel opening and closure, and maintenance of pharyngeal space.

Central to understanding the appropriate pedagogy for crescendo/decrescendo is an accurate definition of the process. While it may be defined as getting "louder" and getting "softer," it will serve pedagogical process better if one considers the crescendo simply as an increase and decrease in resonance.

The overriding problems for most inexperienced choirs is that they execute crescendos and decrescendos without an increase in space, and they fail to maintain spaciousness on the decrescendo and use vowel closure to execute colorful and intense decrescendos. Aligned with this is the problem that forward movement of the air and the entire support apparatus is not maintained.

Before adding the elements of the crescendo/decrescendo, one needs to teach the "air spin" gesture technique presented below:

1. Have the choir move their hands around and forward in a spinning gesture, with the hands rolling over each other.

2. As they perform this gesture, have the choir hiss air using the vowel as if they are saying the word "set." (Note: This ensures the air is being directed in a high and forward position.)

3. When the choir hisses air at a faster speed, then they should move their fingers faster. Similarly, when the air moves slower, they should move their hands slower.

The steps for teaching crescendo/decrescendo to the choir are as follows:

Steps for Teaching Crescendo/Decrescendo

1. Begin moving hands with "air spin" gesture.
2. Begin with the "oo" vowel, with lips "around the sound."
3. As resonance increase is desired, increase pharyngeal space by proper "dropping of the jaw."
4. As resonance increase is desired, increase the airflow **and** the velocity of the hand spin.
5. To execute a decrescendo from the peak of the crescendo, do **not** decrease the speed of the air or the speed of the "air spin" gesture.
6. Allow the vowel to **open** slightly as one increases sound. That is, allow the lips to open slightly, modifying the vowel toward "ah." Be certain the choir does not move toward "uh." Also remember to maintain high, forward placement of the sound at all times.

7. To obtain movement toward a *piano* or *pianissimo* sound resonance, **close** the vowel. That is, wrap the lips around the sound, returning to the original lip position of "oo."
8. When you reach the desired point of the decrescendo, have the choir continue the forward spinning of the hands after the sound is released. This is important because it teaches the choir how to "support" the sound through the decrescendo process and the final release of the sound. Also, by maintaining the forward hand spin, this allows the larynx to stay down during the final release of the sound!

Figure 18 Hand Position for "Air Spin" Gesture

Figure 19 Air Spin Gesture

Range Extension Upward

Because of the technical components necessary to properly sing upward range extension exercises, range extension exercises without technical steps provided for the choir can cause the larynx to rise and result in uncomfortable singing tension within the vocal apparatus. You are encouraged to use the range extension exercises suggested in the **Core Vocal Exercises** later in this book.

Note that the warm-up planning guide suggests that all choral warm-ups must contain range extension exercises. Singing in the upper range is an acquired skill. The vocal technique required must be built over a longer period of time.

Three essential vocal technique elements must be maintained simultaneously if there is to be an extension of the vocal range. First, singing on the breath (support) must be maintained, especially as the voice moves into a higher tessitura. Second, more pharyngeal space must be created as the choir moves higher in their range. Third, if the first two elements are achieved, the third will occur as a healthy by-product. That is, the larynx will be maintained in a low, relaxed position.

Finally, it is important to remind the choir that as the exercise is being sung, the spinal column **lengthens.** Watch for "shortening" of the body as the exercise is being sung.

Vowel Modification and Range Extension

One of the most important principles to understand is that as range increases upward, the vowel must be modified. One of the dangers of many "choral approaches" is that the vowel is not allowed to modify as it ascends. If the vowel modification is not "built in" to this process, then poor vocalism, strident sound, and pitch problems will certainly result. Vowel modification in the upper register is simply an increase in space. As pharyngeal space is increased, or rather "opened," the vowel likewise "opens." Internal space must increase if range extension is to be realized. The arbiter of the sound in this process must be the lips. The lips bring focus and color to the sound in the upper range as the vowel is being changed toward its more open dictional counterpart. Also remember that a correct Body Map of the lips, as presented earlier in this book, is helpful and quite necessary to maintain vowel focus and pitch.

Steps for Teaching Upward Range Extension

1. Always use broken chords or triadic exercises for range extension exercises.

2. Perform range extension exercises at a **fast** tempo.
3. Increase pharyngeal space as the upward range increases.
4. Increase the speed of the air (support) as the exercise ascends.
5. As the exercise ascends, make certain the lips are "wrapped around the sound."
6. Add physical gesture to all range extension exercises so the singers forget where they are going!
7. Make certain the breaths are rhythmic and in the dynamic character of the exercise.
8. Always use an open vowel, such as pure "oh" (with a minimum of diphthong) or "ah." Make certain the lips are wrapped around the sound for these vowels.
9. Make certain all range extension upward exercises begin in the singing part of the voice that is high and forward.

Range Extension Downward

The techniques for teaching range extension downward are opposite of the techniques for teaching range extension upward. Range extension downward must be developed as a separate skill for the choir. While it is an important skill for all sections of the choir, it is very important for voices in the lower registers, that is, the alto and bass/baritone sections.

Downward range extension exercises have the following pedagogical objectives:

1. To bring as much head tone downward from the upper part of the voice into the lower part of the voice; and
2. To teach and reinforce vocal placement that is both **high** and **forward.**

Also, in the initial stages, downward range extension exercises **do not permit any crescendo.** This is a fault of most choirs. They believe that they must increase sound the lower they sing, which causes them to shift into chest register in an unhealthy fashion.

Refer to the **Core Vocal Exercises** later in this book for specific exercises to use in the construction of the ensemble warm-up for downward range extension.

Steps for Teaching Downward Range Extension

1. Always choose a "bright" vowel for these exercises, The preferred vowel is "ee" or the German umlauted "u" (ü).
2. Always perform the exercise at a **slow** tempo.
3. Always move **stepwise** downward. If leaps are contained in the exercise, those leaps can only occur after careful stepwise movement.
4. Maintain **high** and **forward** placement throughout. Use physical gesture (heel of hand on forehead) to ensure proper placement.
5. Do not allow for any crescendo in the exercise.
6. If a crescendo is desired, then achieve that crescendo by **opening** the vowel sound via the lips.

Leaps

Upward leaps pose many problems for the inexperienced singer. Performed without technical help, the innocent leap can compound the singer's difficulties. The most serious problem is that upward leaps inherently cause the singer to "come off the breath," or rather not stay connected to the breath. Another difficulty is that the larynx rises up on the upward leap, which is usually accompanied by a lack of internal pharyngeal space. Add to those difficulties that the vowel usually opens and becomes "spread." One of the most prevalent problems is that the leap begins in the lower register and carries that register upward where there is an absence of head tone. The resultant sound is usually harsh, strident, and loud, especially in the treble voices.

The teaching procedure for proper vocal execution of a leap is as follows:

Teaching Procedure for Leaps

1. Begin the leap with sound that is **high** and **forward.** Choose a bright vowel to begin the exercise.
2. Increase space (the cave) on the upward leap. Use a more spacious vowel sound on the leap.
3. Wrap lips around the sound on the top pitch.

4. Increase the speed of the air **before** the leap occurs, not upon arriving at the upper pitch. (The "air spin" gesture can assist this process.)
5. Use physical gestures to maintain support throughout the leap. (Use the breath "kneading" exercise, including spaciousness.)

Legato

If you have done your work properly to this point, then supported, legato singing should not be a problem. To repair issues with legato, first return to the "breath-kneading" exercise presented earlier (see "Breathing: Teaching 'Support' or 'On the Breath' Singing" in Chapter 9). Constant forward movement of breath is, perhaps, the most serious problem in experienced singers. One can make a great deal of progress with legato by using this technique.

Another reason forward breath flow may be inhibited is because singers have little or no concept of phrase direction of the lines they are attempting to sing. Sometimes, simply pointing out the directionality of phrases will repair problems pertaining to breath flow.

Connected to this problem is a lack of understanding concerning the organic rhythm structure of bar lines. This structure, known as "Note Grouping," is simple but very potent for moving musical line forward. The overriding principle is that the first beat of the bar, regardless of the musical setting, will receive an accent with weight because of the visual power of the bar line that precedes it. Note Grouping pedagogy focuses on minimizing the weight of the first beat of every bar and energizing the portions of the bar that provide for a natural, organic forward movement of the musical line. In most situations, this can be accomplished by simply making the singers aware of the problem and providing some ground rules as follows:

Note Grouping Rules for Internal Musical Phrasing

- Energize all rests through rhythmic breath that is energized and propels the subsequent phrase.
- In a bar that groups itself into four beats, energize beats two and three. "Let go" of beats four and one. Be careful **never** to accent or bring undue weight onto beat one.

- In a bar that groups itself into three beats, energize the second beat only. Be careful not to accent or bring undue weight onto beat one.
- To assist in withholding weight and accent from beat one, have the choir sing the longest vowel possible, and then have consonants occur quickly and immediately **after** the beat.
- To foster understanding of the kinesthetic of musical line, have the choir "moan" the line.
- Weak beats should move to strong beats.
- Short beats should move to long beats.
- Repeated notes should change their character.
- All rests should be energized.

The Kinesthetic of Vocalic Flow

Legato is manifest in singers as vocalic flow—that is, the ongoing forward movement of the vowel that carries sound. This vocalic flow is the organic core of a well-sung musical line. What makes this an elusive concept for singers is that the kinesthetic, or body feeling of what it feels like to sing a musical line, must be taught. It is that kinesthetic singers will remember, which will result in the union of many sophisticated concepts that are involved with singing musical line.

If one examines the true nature of a musical line and reduces it to kinesthetic feeling, that kinesthetic feeling is the organic or basic core of a musical line. The musical line is a connection with oneself and one's energy and belief core that can, in turn, propel sound forward. Moreover, musical line is a primal part of our musical being; it is basic to all musical expression.

The most efficient way to gain an ensemble's understanding of this sophisticated idea is to have the choir moan the musical line on a monotone pitch using the consonants "mmmmmm." When done correctly, one should hear an uninterrupted forward movement of sound. The resonance of that sound should increase with the rises in the musical line. Most importantly, however, one should **never** be aurally aware of the bar lines when the choir is moaning. If bar lines are heard, then this is an indication that support is not continuously engaged and a forward direction in the choir's cognitive awareness is not in place. Put another way, there needs to be a constant and omnipresent **awareness** of the entire body for legato line to be energized and forward moving. Without that awareness, there can be no compelling musical line that is artistic and expressive because it lacks connection in the most fundamental way to each singer. There is no more formidable enemy of musical line than a lack of awareness on the part of the singer!

Finally, diction principles are important for the aural manifestation of line. Simply stated, vowels must be as long as possible, and consonants must be as short as possible. Consonants should also not carry undue weight into the subsequent vowel sounds.

Techniques for Teaching and Reinforcing Legato Line

1. Use the breath "kneading" gesture to continually reinforce the connection of forward-moving breath to vocalic flow.
2. Have the choir "moan" the line.
3. Continually remind the choir to be in a constant state of awareness. The singers must be aware of their entire body as they sing.
4. Make certain the choir understands where each musical phrase moves toward (e.g., text stresses, etc.).
5. Use physical movement whenever possible to reinforce the kinesthetic of the line. Make the musical line a physical experience!
6. In situations where the vowel is repeated on repeated pitches or in running passages, ask the singers to "re-sing" the vowel on every pitch.

Staccato Singing: Does It Exist for Singers?

Clarification is needed concerning the use of the term "staccato singing." To start, staccato as it exists in instrumental music does not exist in quite the same form in vocal music. The "dry" staccatos that can be executed by an oboe simply cannot be replicated in singers. Articulation in choral ensembles is always related directly to the dictional demands of the text. But the range of staccato articulation in singers is limited. In fact, it is best not to employ the word "staccato" in one's teaching of singers. The use of the word usually brings undue pressure upon the larynx and tends to upset or break the vocalic flow. In most situations, staccato singing in its truest sense is not what is desired. Rather, what is desired is a lighter, more buoyant approach to the musical materials. If a more articulated style is needed, then use the techniques for teaching martellato that are explained in the next section.

Martellato

Martellato is an articulation term that is understood in the instrumental world but has had a relatively new life with respect to vocal music. As was stated in the prior section, it is not particularly accurate to use the term "staccato" when referring to passages that require a shorter articulation. Martellato is an articulation that is midway between legato and staccato. It is especially useful in articulating running passages, especially in Baroque and Classical literature.

Compromise Techniques

The technique presented here is a compromise procedure designed to allow inexperienced singers to sing passages that might normally be outside their technical abilities. In the most ideal situation, it would be desirable if the singers have enough muscular control of the breath mechanism to allow for breath to be maintained while the vowel is re-articulated on the running notes. For most choirs, this is not possible. Consequently, techniques that provide the basal level of skills needed to sing such passages can be of great use.

There is a technique that can be employed, especially with large choirs. This technique—**use of the repeated "d"**—is especially useful when trying to bring clarity to dense contrapuntal passages.

1. On passages that have extended runs, divide the choir in half.

2. Have half of the choir sing the runs without any consonants, merely repeating the vowel on each note of the run.

3. Have the other half of the choir sing the same passage but insert the consonant "d" on each pitch of the run. This is a bit of an

acoustic trick. The insertion of the consonant "d" will not be heard in the hall. Rather, a clean articulation of the run will be heard.

4. If further rhythmic clarity of the run is desired, then increase the numbers of singers singing "d."

Teaching Martellato

The steps that follow (see "Steps for Teaching Martellato") should be used in teaching martellato singing technique to the choir. Pedagogically, there are several approaches that work well. One technique is to simply extract a run from the passage of music being rehearsed and apply the teaching technique detailed below to that passage. Another technique is to introduce martellato with the exercise below. Every time a piece of music requires martellato, the same exercise should be used to "reawaken" the martellato technique taught earlier. Because singing martellato is a kinesthetic experience, the choir can generally make the transfer of the technique easily within the same rehearsal. It is important, however, to insist on two guidelines with the choir when applying martellato to the literature.

1. The choir should place horizontal tenuto dashes with dots over them over each note of the run.

2. If the run is on one syllable of text, the choir should write the repeated vowel sound under **each** note. This second step is most important because inexperienced singers tend to forget what vowel they are singing on the run. The vowel on such runs usually morphs into some form of "uh," which is not desirable! It is important throughout the run to re-think and/or re-sing the vowel on each pitch.

Use of Pointing to Assist in Gaining Textural Clarity

In addition to the martellato technique presented in the next section, a rehearsal technique involving pointing is very useful to bring both clarity to the overall texture and clarity of vowel to the texture. For each note of the run, have the choir point on each note. Pointing immediately brings clarity to the attack of each pitch and minimizes or eliminates glissandi between pitches. It is such glissandi between pitches that bring textural disclarity and inaccurate pitch to choral ensembles. Remember that the larger the choir, the more one must minimize such glissandi in the texture. The correct area for pointing is shown below. Some rules for pointing also follow:

1. **Point high and forward.** Pointing in the upward direction of the cheekbones and forehead in front of the face is central to this technique. If the pointing occurs in this area, sufficient head tone will be maintained in the vocal sound.

2. **Point with a minimum of weight: point by withholding weight.** Aside from purely technical reasons, one of the reasons choirs are unable to sing running passages is that there is simply too much "weight" in the choral sound. When the choir points, have them imagine that they are "dabbing" each note; that is, have them imagine that they are repeatedly dotting the letter "i" on each note of the run. If the texture is still too heavy, then have the choir imagine that they are dabbing watercolor onto a canvas with a brush for each note. For further clarification of this teaching technique, see Chapter 16, which explains the use of Laban to assist with vocal technique and musical style.

3. **Make certain each pointing gesture is released.** If pointing is used as a technique, it is very important that the hand releases backward without any weight after each point because forward motion of the breath stream must be maintained on the run. If the hand does not release backward, then the singer is "locking" or "holding" the breath during the running passage. By focusing the singers on their physical gesture, vocal technique can be corrected efficiently, quickly, and without intimidation.

Teaching Procedure for Pointing for Martellato and Textural Clarification

1. Always point high and forward.
2. Point with a minimum of weight: point by withholding weight.
3. Make certain each pointing gesture is released.

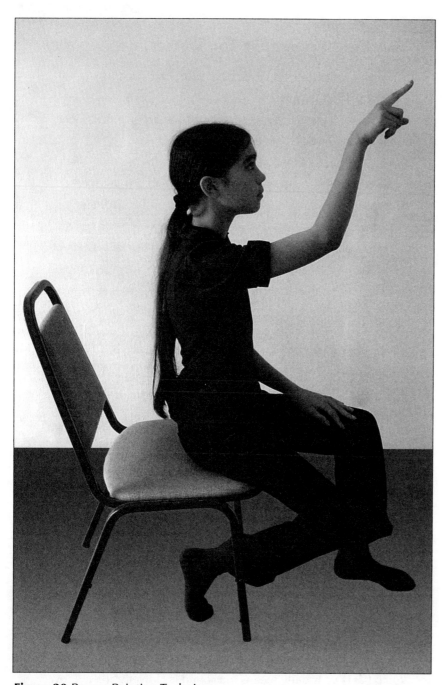

Figure 20 Proper Pointing Technique

Steps for Teaching Martellato

Use the following exercise for teaching martellato. This exercise can be found in the **Core Vocal Exercises** section of this text.

Teaching Procedure for Martellato

1. Exercise in triplets: SLS FSF MFM RMR D.
2. Sing SFMRD in quarter notes at a slow tempo on the syllable "dah." With each repeated "dah," drop the jaw in an exaggerated fashion on each pitch and accent each note.
3. Now sing SLS FSF MFM RMR D on the syllable "dah" placed on **each** note at a slow tempo, still with the jaw dropped.
4. Increase the tempo. Remove the second and third "dah." Reduce the dynamic. Reduce the jaw drop.
5. Increase the tempo again. Remove all "dah" syllables except for the first. Reduce the dynamic. Minimize the jaw dropping to almost nothing; transform into a relaxed jaw. Be sure to repeat the vowel on each note! Use pointing to clarify the texture.

Teaching Diction through the Choral Warm-Up

One of the most important sections of both the choral ensemble warm-up and the choral rehearsal is an efficient strategy for teaching diction. Stated another way, specific teaching techniques must be employed by the conductor to assist the choir in understanding the transition between spoken diction and sung diction. Without the help of specific techniques, despite the most intricately planned rehearsal technique, if the introduction of text is not handled in a pedagogically efficient manner, then diction can sabotage most, if not all, of one's work in the rehearsal. The choral profession has generally embraced the philosophy that all one needs to do is to "speak the text after me." There are generally no steps that assist the choir in understanding the **feeling** of singing text in a vocal way. Without that instruction, the singers tend to default to the way they speak language. For vocal purposes, that usually means the sound is "jowelly" (i.e., a low "throaty" placement) and the vowels are generally too open to maintain appropriate choral color and/or pitch.

Exercises that incorporate the text of the works being rehearsed should be included in the second portion of the choral warm-up. A six-step procedure should **always** be used when introducing and teaching diction to the choir (see "Six-Step Diction Teaching Technique"). Remember that throughout these six steps, the sound must always remain **spacious, high, and forward.** These techniques should provide assistance with maintaining the proper sound.

Choosing the Appropriate Vowel Color

Note of caution: Determine the amount of vowel closure necessary to achieve the appropriate choral style. Before any diction teaching begins, it is important to determine the amount of vowel closure necessary to achieve both the desired choral sound and the stylistic appropriateness of the sound. For most inexperienced choirs, one cannot err on the side of overly closing the vowel when teaching a text. The reason for this logic is that, in general, the choir will only do approximately half of what you ask them to do!

Musical style in choral music is achieved through diction. An understanding of the language being sung with respect to vowel color and consonant execution can be gleaned from a basic understanding of speaking characteristics of the language. To gain an understanding of the speaking characteristics, answer the following questions for each piece and the language employed for the piece.

> ### Steps for Choosing Appropriate Diction Vowel Color
>
> 1. What typifies the vowel color of this language?
> 2. How are consonants executed in this language?
> 3. What is the color of the stylistic period of this music?
> 4. What is the color of the sound the composer heard?

1. **What typifies the vowel color of this language?** Are the vowels taller and narrower, or are they rounder?

2. **How are consonants executed in this language?** Are the consonants executed quickly? Do the consonants interrupt the vocalic flow, or do they merely ride upon it? How much weight do the consonants carry into the vowels that follow?

3. **What is the color of the stylistic period of this music?** What is the style color of the musical period of which this music is a part? What influence does this have upon the language, if any? As a general rule, both the style of the language and the musical style of the period must be taken into consideration. In most situations, the style of the language will have an overriding influence upon the style. For example, although Faure is considered in the romantic style period, the performance of his music must express a French language viewpoint.

4. **What is the color of the sound the composer heard?** This is a controversial point, however one that must be considered seriously. It has been my experience that if this question has not been reconciled in the mind of the conductor/teacher, the music is never really allowed to "sing." An example is the Faure *Requiem*. The piece is in Latin, and Faure was a French composer. Is it not possible that Faure heard Latin but in a French style? If one performs the Faure *Requiem* with Italianate Latin, the choral sound is generally too thick and heavy. The beautiful musical lines of Faure do not scan forward to the end of the phrase (as does the French language), but rather get stuck on overly weighted, heavy consonants.

Color decisions are inherent in every language sung. What is the appropriate color for the German language? What is the appropriate color for English sung in a British style? If performing the music of Haydn, should one use church Latin or, rather, Latin sung in a German style. These decisions are crucially important for choral performance, regardless of the level of the choir. Many conductors expend needless time and effort in an attempt to achieve a musical style solely through the music without using the most important helper in achieving musical style—diction.

Six-Step Diction Teaching Technique

Below are listed the six steps for teaching diction to a choral ensemble. The introduction of diction should always occur during the warm-up procedure, apart from the musical part of the rehearsal. Elements of diction must be prepared before they are placed with the musical materials.

Moreover, when taught in this way, a careful transition from speaking diction to singing diction will occur.

All the steps below may be contained in a single warm-up, but it is more desirable to view the six steps as independent steps that are best introduced one at a time in separate rehearsals. Done in this way, the effect of the teaching is cumulative and has time to be both absorbed and experienced by the choir. It should also be noted that these steps are presented in their pedagogical hierarchical order. That is, sustained speech should not be taught until the technique of correct speech is taught.

After the choir has been introduced to the text with Technique 1, you may begin to sing the music you are rehearsing with text.

Technique 1: Correct Speech
Speak the text correctly to the choir in the rhythm of the piece. The speech employed should be spacious, high, and forward. Using speech in this style will begin the transition from spoken diction to sung diction.

Technique 2: Sustained Speech
Speak the text to the choir out of the rhythm of the piece in a slow, sustained style that is still spacious, high, and forward. The importance of this technique is that in speaking in a sustained fashion, one must sustain vowels over a longer period of time and then change to the next vowel. Inexperienced choirs usually begin moving toward the next vowel while they are sustaining the previous vowel. This technique ensures that singers maintain the same vowel over an extended time period. Viewed from a technical point of view, this technique ensures that there is no change in the tongue position as the vowel is being sustained.

Technique 3: Heightened Exaggerated Speech
This technique is often referred to as the "Mrs. Doubtfire" technique. Ask the choir to speak the text in a heightened, spacious, exaggerated style, almost imitating an exaggerated, spacious British accent. When the choir speaks the text in this way, they can feel what it is like to sing text with spaciousness. Listen to be certain the spaciousness of the speech does not diminish between words of the text as the choir moves from vowel to vowel via consonants. If this occurs, it is an indication that the consonants are too long, too weighted, or both.

Technique 4: Staccato Singing on Text
After you have drilled the choir using heightened, exaggerated speech,

you generally will find that the sound of the choir improves greatly. Maintaining the newly found spaciousness, however, is a challenge! One of the most valuable techniques for assisting with this is to have the choir sing the piece on the text, but sing everything shortened or quasi-staccato. This is an effective technique for two important reasons.

First, most pitch and diction problems occur in a choir because singers are uncertain of the vowel they are to sing on each pitch they sing. Consequently, when singing, they "adjust" or "morph" the vowel once they sing the pitch. The aural manifestation of this is a fluctuation of pitch and choral color that is in a constant state of flux. By singing staccato, singers are forced to commit to the correct vowel on the attack. When they do not, **they** can hear it manifest as poor pitch in the ensemble sound that surrounds them.

Second, by singing in a quasi-staccato style, the break or air space between each pitch allows the choir time to **hear** the next pitch and the next vowel, thus ensuring more accurate pitch and rhythm.

To further add pedagogical potency to this procedure, the addition of an aural metronome coalesces and homogenizes choral sound quickly by eliminating human rhythmic hesitation on the part of the singers. This procedure also ensures that there is a quick and efficient change between and among all vowel sounds and that consonants are handled with quick dispatch.

Technique 5: Voweling

Voweling is a technique that further solidifies quick changes between vowel sounds. With this technique, ask the choir to sing vowel sounds only without consonants.

This technique further refines the necessary skill of quickly and efficiently changing vowel sounds. As stated above, the use of an aural metronome can hasten and clarify the quickness of these vowel changes by eliminating the factor of human hesitation. The clicking of the metronome forces the choir to quickly move to the next vowel sound without hesitation.

Technique 6: Whole-Tone Chordal Singing

This technique was a favorite of the late Robert Shaw. Using this technique, build a chord of four whole tones, each tone being assigned to a different voice part in the choir. Have the choir chant the rhythm of the piece you are rehearsing on the whole-tone chord. If the chord goes out of tune or changes color, then the only responsible culprit is the vowel. It is then the choir's responsibility to adjust the vowel accordingly.

Teaching Pieces That Are Highly Rhythmic

While the above six-step process is preferred for teaching diction to a choir, there are some pieces that are best taught from the beginning stages with their texts intact: pieces where the rhythm of the piece **is** the text. With such pieces, pitch and the inherent organic rhythm of the piece are so bound together that it is unwise to separate them in the teaching process.

When encountering such pieces, teach the text in the rhythm of the piece but on unison repeated pitch, or use the whole-tone chordal singing technique (Technique 6) listed above. Throughout the rehearsal process, use the other diction teaching techniques to further polish the diction. Remember at all times to make sure the sounds made by the choir are always **spacious, high,** and **forward.**

Vowel Correction Hierarchy

Order of Vowel and Consonant Correction

1. "OO" and "EE"
2. Elimination of Diphthongs
3. "AH"
4. "EH" and "IH"
5. Execution of Consonants Appropriate to Style

Many conductors, especially young and inexperienced ones make the mistake of trying to correct everything at once! By employing such a tactic, they hopelessly confuse the choir, and very little long-term correction of diction takes place. I have found that many ensemble diction problems occur because the "oo" and "ee'" vowels are not sung pure and clear.

As you listen to the choir sing using the techniques presented above, first correct the "oo" and "ee" vowels. There are several important reasons for this. First, the "oo" and "ee" vowels are the vowels that carry and maintain head tone in the sound. Without these vowels, choral sound becomes dull and pitch problems also usually abound. When the "oo" and "ee" vowels are not clear, then there is insufficient head tone carried into the other vowels that surround these sounds. Second, the "oo" and "ee" vowels are problematic for singers because they require a change of tongue position and a slight modification of the shape of the lips. This mechanical process is necessary for vowel clarity. Inexperienced choirs usually manage to sing both vowels with the same tongue position and merely get some degree of vowel change by adjusting their lips! By focusing the choir on the correct execution of the pure "ee" and pure "oo," this will correct many diction problems within the choir.

After all "oo" and "ee" vowels are being sung with reasonable clarity and resonance, then begin correcting other vowels, again in a hierarchical order. The next vowel that should be corrected is "ah." Make certain the "ah" vowel is spacious, high, and forward. Sometimes, applying physical gesture to encourage a high and forward placement of the sound is most efficient. Make certain the "ah" vowel is not defaulting toward the neutral "uh" sound, which is a "jowel vowel" and suffers for lack of forward and high placement.

Next, correct the "ih" and "eh" vowels. These vowels usually suffer from a lack of vowel closure and sound to the ear as "spread" or too open. When the vowel lacks sufficient closure, you generally cannot hear the core of the pitch being sung with any clarity. Ask the choir to "wrap their lips around the sound" to bring more focus to these vowels.

If problems still persist, it is usually because of the consonant that precedes the vowel. A poorly articulated consonant will twist or damage the vowel sound that follows. Correct the articulation of these troublesome consonants either by incorporating them into a warm-up specially designed for the choir or by correcting the articulation with suggestions from the book by Madeline Marshall, *English Diction,* published by G. Schirmer.

Interdependent Relationship and Pedagogy of the "oo" and "ee" Vowels

As stated earlier in this text, the "oo" and "ee" vowels are the most important vowels for building a healthy choral sound. Once the vowels have been introduced and are being clearly phonated, then it is necessary to further define the color of the vowel. Without correction, the "oo" vowel sung by most choirs generally lacks color and pitch core because the vowel is sung too far back and does not utilize the maximum resonential spaces possible. The "ee" vowel is generally sung too "open" and is overly bright because of a lack of vertical spaciousness. Hence, to build healthy "oo" and "ee" vowels, the "oo" vowel must contain elements of "ee," and the "ee" vowel must contain elements of "oo." To achieve this, the following must be done:

1. For the "oo" vowel, ask the choir to imagine that there is an "ee" vowel behind the "oo" vowel. By asking them to do this, the "oo" will be infused with a bit more "brightness" that will clarify the pitch core of the "oo" vowel.

2. For the "ee" vowel, ask the choir to "wrap their lips around the sound" and imagine that there is an "oo" vowel behind their sung "ee" vowel. By asking the choir to do this, the "ee" vowel will be infused with a bit more of the quality of the "oo" vowel. By doing this, a rounder, more spacious "ee" vowel will be the result.

While I realize that building both vowels in this manner in many ways eliminates the pure "oo" vowel and the pure "ee" vowel, those vowels in their purest forms cannot blend in a choral situation because of a lack of overtones that, in turn, allow for blend to occur. The "oo" vowel generally suffers from a lack of pitch core, and the "ee" vowel is generally too strident. By approaching the "oo" and "ee" vowels in this manner, you will find the choir produces more beautiful vowel sounds that more naturally blend without further effort.

Basic Diction Pitfalls

There are many books written that clarify the intricacies of sung diction. However, for the purposes of basic choral pedagogy, the vigilance over several problems will correct the major diction stumbling blocks for most choirs.

The Schwa

Of all diction problems, this one is perhaps the most prevalent among choirs. By definition, **a schwa is an unaccented or unstressed neutral syllable.** In choral performance, these syllables must be muted. Schwas can take many visual forms, and they can occupy positions within words at the end, beginning, or middle of words. There may also be more than one schwa within a word.

There is also a secondary form of a schwa: a syllable that needs to be muted because of dialect.

The schwa is indicated in the examples below by boldface type.

moth**er** (omit the "r")	fath**er** (omit the "r")
heav**en**	**di**vine
remem**brance**	nev**er** (omit the "r")
low**est**	child**ren**
corn**er**	op**en**
ap**ple**	lit**tle**

Follow the procedure below for all schwas.

Teaching Schwas

1. Identify the syllable in the word that is a schwa.
2. Have the choir circle the schwa syllable in red.
3. Ask the choir to wrap their lips around the sound for the syllable that has been identified as the schwa.
4. Make sure the lips participate in the muting (unstressing) of the schwa.
5. Be certain the schwa sound does not become dark in color. Schwa sounds must also be spacious, high, and forward. Always maintain the internal color and integrity of the vowel.

Diphthongs

Diphthongs are syllables within words whose sound is composed of two vowel sounds. In solo singing, the instruction for diphthongs is to merely slip the second vowel in before moving to the next vowel sound.

However, in a choral ensemble, if a singer or a number of singers slip in the second vowel prematurely, the overall aural effect will be heard as poor intonation! Consequently, it is important to minimize or "eliminate" diphthongs in choral singing so as not to interfere with good pitch. Some examples of diphthongs are as follows:

day	night	play	toy	voice
home	my	soul	eyes	loud
fine	came	light		

To correct the problem of diphthongs within a choral situation, ask the choir to sing only the first vowel and eliminate the second vowel altogether. **The acoustical reality is that the choir will insert the vowel at the appropriate time as they move to the next word.** It is also important that the jaw remains in the position of the first vowel of the diphthong throughout the singing of the word.

The Troublesome "R"

The consonant "r" is extremely troublesome for American choirs. The problem is that, without instruction, Americans often sing the "reflexive American r." The "r" sung in this way is extremely damaging to the vowel that follows for two reasons. First, the American "r" usually sends the sound backward in the throat, and second, the "r" tends to twist or distort the vowel sound that immediately follows. To eliminate this problem, never sing an "r" before a consonant and single flip or roll an "r" when it occurs before a vowel.

The Tip of the Tongue "L"

For American choirs, this consonant is problematic because its American pronunciation ensures the placement of the sound in the mid or rear mouth. To eliminate this problem, ask the choir to articulate the "l" with the tip of the tongue contacting the area just above the upper teeth gum line.

The following resources are recommended for specific diction problems:

Marshall, Madeline. *English Diction.* New York: G. Schirmer.

For diction in specific styles and style periods:

McGee, Timothy J. *Singing Early Music: The Pronunciation of European Languages in the Late Middle Ages and Renaissance.* Bloomington: Indiana University Press, 1996.

Also consult the diction resources listed in the Bibliography at the back of this book.

PART V

AURAL IMMERSION AND AURAL PREPARATION OF THE CHOIR

Chapter 12
Aural Immersion and Aural Preparation of the Choir

At the end of the warm-up sequence, time should be allotted to teach music skill to the choir. This subject is addressed in detail in *Ear Training Immersion Exercises for Choirs* (GIA, 2004). It is important that the tonality or tonalities to be sung at the rehearsal are prepared aurally. That is, the choir should sing in Dorian, Phrygian, minor, etc., before attempting to sing the choral literature.

Since writing *Choral Ensemble Intonation* (GIA, 2001), I experienced a swift learning curve concerning the concepts presented in *Ear Training Immersion Exercises for Choirs* (GIA). I am convinced of the power of learning a piece of music while being immersed at all times in its harmonic surroundings. Since the publication of the book, I have been amazed at how quickly choirs can learn pieces—even difficult pieces—using this approach.

However, as I have conducted workshops on these materials, participants have asked for teaching materials that are usable for choirs at all levels of development and all levels of experience. More importantly, I have discovered how important it is for harmonic information to be provided at all times to singers.

For years I was taught—and believed—that choirs could be taught to hear better through unison singing. Hence, my warm-ups and "part teaching" were done unison, many times with a skeletal piano accompaniment. I am now convinced through experience that a choir's aural literacy grows exponentially by supplying harmonic materials at all times. I have found that one's harmonic surroundings provide many aural clues for context that are quite powerful. I have also found that not to provide such surroundings allows for rampant aural speculation on the part of the singers. **Harmonic context is everything.** Harmonic context provides many aural links for the musician by providing context for what is being heard. The power of that context has been underestimated in the design of musicianship materials, especially those written for choral ensembles. The reasons for this are many, and hopefully this will be the focus of future experimental research.

Throughout this process, I have also marveled at the power of the dominant function note in any mode. The sounding of the dominant gives **immediate** aural organization to the musical materials so they can be learned and understood. Its power cannot and should not be underestimated. Although the sounding of the resting tone provides some beginning aural information and begins to focus the ear, it is only when the dominant is sounded in alternation with the resting tone that the syntax of the tonality is aurally identified and organized in the performers' ears.

Consistent with those two points—(1) the importance of harmonic immersion at all times and (2) the aural organizational power of the dominant and the resting tone—materials have been written for this teaching manual that incorporate these pivotal ideas. It must be cautioned, however, that these materials should not be used until the user has read *Choral Ensemble Intonation* (GIA) and viewed the accompanying video.

Basic Assumptions

1. **Aptitude testing is a must.** Basic assumptions proposed in *Choral Ensemble Intonation* are still intact. Aptitude testing using the tests of Edwin Gordon (GIA) is still at the core of this instruction. Knowing how well the choir can hear or audiate allows you to pace instruction appropriately and select materials for performance that the choir can **hear.**

2. **Understand what your choir really hears.** While this may sound like a radical statement, many persons in your choir hear **only in major.** Consequently, their entire musical life is spent associating all the music they perform with major to make it aurally understandable to them. Although there will be a few singers who bring more to the musical table than just major, the vast majority of singers aurally sift all the music they try to learn through a major "filter." Because of this, the root of most severe intonation problems lies in an inability on the part of the singers to establish the appropriate context for learning. That context is the **mode** and its inherent **harmonic implications.** Without modal **syntax,** there can be little or no long-term musical learning or understanding.

3. **Supply aural anchors whenever possible, both in warm-up procedures and the rehearsal process.** The power of supplying the dominant

function **above** what the choir is singing is of singular importance. By supplying the dominant in a tessitura that can be easily perceived, the resting tone of the mode can be—and is—inferred. When the resting tone of the mode and the dominant are clearly established, real music learning rather than inappropriate types of rote learning can take place. When these aural anchors are not supplied, the singers unknowingly and naively engage passive rather than active listening strategies.

4. **Surround singers at all times with the harmonic richness and unique qualities of each mode.** Edwin Gordon has proven beyond doubt the importance of the **aural oral** level of learning for musicians. Singers should be provided with materials to **hear.** The choices for what the singers hear are both profound and far-reaching with respect to their musical development. It follows that all materials presented to singers must be of the highest musical level. I have found that it is a mistake to simply dismiss or ignore the vocalizing process or moments during the rehearsal that have traditionally yielded to unison singing. It is at these times that a great deal of aural musical information can be supplied to the singers through appropriately harmonized exercises. This, perhaps, was the over-riding objective of *Ear Training Immersion Exercises for Choirs* (GIA).

5. **Do not underestimate the power of solfege syllables sung within a harmonic environment.** There is incredible aural power lodged within the internal logic of solfege syllables. Solfege, when sung not as unisons but within a sounded harmonic sea, appears to establish **immediate** context for the singers, regardless of experience level. This cannot be emphasized enough. It is this concept that sets this approach to ensemble aural literacy apart from other approaches. Neutral syllable singing is encouraged first to point the way. But it is solfege and its magical inherent logic that solidifies music learning at the most basic level. The use of solfege also allows for the orderly organization of aural musical material, providing that a movable "do" system is employed. Fixed "do" systems and other systems require the singers to have a sophisticated level of theoretical musical understanding before they can begin performing music with any degree of understanding.

6. **Materials are presented in *Ear Training Immersion Exercises for Choirs* (GIA) based on hearing or audiating difficulty level.** It should be noted that the modes are presented in that text in their order of difficulty. **This is done not to prescribe a curriculum of instruction, but rather to allow the conductor to realize that certain modes are more difficult to hear and may require more teaching and learning time than others.** This information has been established through extensive research in the work of Edwin Gordon. For further information, consult his books on Music Learning Theory listed in the bibliography of this book. This hierarchy should be kept in mind at all times.

7. **Move the choir ensemble from passive audiation to active audiation.** Without harmonic immersion, a choral ensemble audiates passively—that is, they hear the music but for many reasons focus only on their part and learn it devoid of context (both harmonic and musical context). When a rich harmonic environment is provided at all times in addition to the dominant function, the choir moves from passively audiating without musical understanding to a level of active audiation, where harmonic context is established through active listening—that is, listening to everything else except themselves.

8. **The dominant function note in any mode can never be assumed to be audiated by a choral ensemble.** Mature and experienced musicians naturally audiate the dominant function note. This audiation of the dominant has been assumed to also occur in less-skilled musicians. This is not the case. In the early stages of musical learning, the dominant must be constantly supplied aurally to the singers via the keyboard. Singers must be taught to listen for this "note." Through repetition, audiation of the dominant will be acquired and become omnipresent in the singers' audiation.

9. **Change and transform the depth of singers' listening.** Central to the materials presented in *Choral Ensemble Intonation* (GIA) is the concept of depth and intensity of listening. For any musical learning to take place, musicians must understand that they need to listen in a starkly different way than they listen in life. Their listening, using an art analogy, must move from minimally contrasted black and white to brilliant color. They must learn to listen to everything.

They must be guided to listening awareness at profound levels. This concept and philosophy is called **aware audiation.**

Despite the simplicity of the melodic materials, the materials presented in *Ear Training Immersion Exercises for Choirs* (GIA) were designed to provide choral ensembles with harmonically rich musical exercises that have built into their composition the dominant function ostinato. Examples for all modes are presented, including the octatonic scale. To assist moving between modalities and keyalities, many composers present the octatonic scale as a possible mode because of its harmonic ambidexterity and its use.

In an effort to demonstrate applications of these principles to performance literature, *Ear Training Immersion Exercises for Choirs* (GIA) contains examples of how music can be aurally presented to the choir. For each mode, the following exercises are presented:

- **Intonation in mode** – used to establish general harmonic context
- **Intervals within mode** – exercises that allow the choir to hear intervals in the harmonic context of the mode
- **Modal tuning exercises** – exercises that allow the choir to navigate tuning the mode through active listening and singing
- **Modal choral examples** – examples supplied to demonstrate applications to the choral literature

There is a published Singer's Edition for these exercises. This is a must for ensembles that truly would like to benefit from this approach. It is important that students see what they are hearing. When taught in this way, reading becomes a by-product of the listening process. In effect, choirs will begin to read without encumbering themselves with extensive music theory required in most approaches to begin music reading. Sounds in this approach are always associated with the signs rather than the symbols of those sounds.

Pedagogical Sequencing of Immersion Exercises

For each of the tonalities, the following exercises are presented in *Ear Training Immersion Exercises for Choirs* (GIA, 2004).

- An intonation exercise
- An interval exercise or exercises
- A tuning or aural warm-up exercise
- Representative examples from the choral literature

The accompaniments in that volume must be played exactly as notated. Omission of parts or re-harmonization of these exercises will diminish the potency of the exercises. Special care must be taken to observe this rule in all the exercises, but especially in the modal exercises.

Audiational Warning

The exercises in *Ear Training Immersion Exercises for Choirs* (GIA) should not be undertaken until each student has performed in solo for the teacher the pattern drills suggested in *Choral Ensemble Intonation* and contained in Octavo #G-55271 (GIA).

Cautionary Note

If ensembles have difficulty performing any of the tasks requested in *Ear Training Immersion Exercises for Choirs* (GIA), it is recommended that pattern training be undertaken, as detailed by Edwin Gordon in the *Jump Right In* music series (GIA, 2002). An inability to perform the musical tasks in *Ear Training Immersion Exercises for Choirs* (GIA) indicates that there is not sufficient aural readiness for the singers to hear and musically understand what they are hearing. The pattern training should emphasize the aural/oral level of learning and the verbal association level of learning. The tonalities of major, minor, Mixolydian, and Dorian should be explored using these materials. And none of these materials should be used unless a standardized measure of music aptitude has been administered (*Advanced Measures of Music Audiation*, GIA).

General Teaching Procedure

1. After the vocal technique section of the warm-up is completed, then make sure students notice in their performance edition the **tonality** they are about to sing and its construction.

2. At this point, it may be helpful to remind singers to listen to everything else except themselves to promote aware audiation.

3. Have the students sing all exercises on the neutral syllable first. For legato passages, "noo" is the preferred syllable; however, "nee" should be used for more accurate pitch. For non-legato passages, "du" is the syllable of choice. Never use any other syllables!

4. After one or two repetitions with the neutral syllable, move to solfege syllables, as suggested in *Choral Ensemble Intonation* (GIA). Make certain the solfege syllables are sung with sufficient vowel closure to ensure accurate pitch via a good pitch core.

5. Never sing the exercises without the accompaniments. Be certain to include the dominant function ostinato as notated in the examples.

6. Return to the neutral syllable when intonation has stabilized to ensure there is sufficient musical line.

7. Begin each exercise with a rhythmic breath in the value of the "beat" or "pulse" of the piece. Breathe in the unit of beat that you would walk to when performing the piece.

Specific Teaching Procedures for Each Category of Exercises

Intonation Exercises

1. These exercises must be sounded and sung prior to the rehearsal of the choral literature. This can occur either during the end of the warm-up for the rehearsal or immediately prior to rehearsal of the piece.
2. Sing the intonation exercises first in unison with neutral syllable "noo."
3. Repeat the exercises with solfege syllables in unison.
4. Sing the exercises in four parts with solfege syllables.

Extended Intonation Exercises for Each Tonality

1. Make certain the students notice the modality of the scale, either through your announcement or their reading of the information at the top of the score.

2. Sing the exercises first on neutral syllable.
3. Proceed to solfege syllables as printed. Make sure vowels are adequately closed to ensure accurate pitch.
4. Use pointing if necessary, as demonstrated on the *Choral Ensemble Intonation* video.

Interval Exercises

With these exercises, it is important to establish accurate intonation within the tonality the choir is singing. Perform interval exercises only after an intonation exercise has been sung.

1. Listen to the voice part played with the accompaniment.
2. Sing the exercise in unison with solfege syllables.
3. Make certain the aural anchors in the accompaniment are supplied in all readings of the exercises.
4. On exercises that use leaps, make certain to minimize glissando by asking the choir to point on the attach of each note.
5. On repetitions of the exercise, reinforce having the choir listen to the keyboard part more than they listen to themselves.

Chapter 13

Blending through Standings and Rehearsal Room Chair Arrangements

Perhaps no single technique available to a conductor can produce as dramatic and far-reaching effects as adjusting the seating arrangement of a choral ensemble to maximize both the acoustic of the rehearsal room and the overtone series of the voices within the choir. Many pitch and "blend" issues are the result of a lack of careful seating arrangements designed for the choir. It can be said that good choral blend and good pitch cannot be achieved without some seating adjustment.

There is another more important reason, however, why acoustic standings need to be incorporated into the rehearsal process. If seating arrangements are not created with the overtone series of the voices as the primary objective, vocal damage could result. Without an acoustic standing procedure, it is virtually impossible for voices, especially larger voices, to sing freely. If not seated in an acoustical setting that will maximize specific overtone series, the larger voices are often accused of "not blending" or even singing out of tune. All of this can be avoided by carefully considering how to arrange the singers within your choir.

Pros and Cons of Scattered Quartet Standings

Many conductors use what are commonly referred to as quartet standings or singing in quartets. There are many advantages to such an arrangement, although the author prefers the arrangements that are used in this book over quartet seatings. While quartet seatings accomplish the objective of "opening up" the choral sound by spreading larger voices throughout the choir and enhancing the need to listen more carefully, it is more difficult for the conductor to influence the musical issues of the music when voice parts are spread throughout the choir. A quartet standing is certainly a desirable rehearsal strategy to heighten both attention and listening within a rehearsal.

The quartet standing attributed to Robert Shaw is actually a radical misinterpretation of what Mr. Shaw intended for this arrangement. According to Weston Noble in *Achieving Choral Blend through Standing Position*

(DVD, GIA Publications, 2005), Robert Shaw stood his choir **vertically**—not **horizontally** as the quartet standing procedure folklore suggests. Many choral conductors believe the "quartet scatter" technique was to stand the entire choir in equally matched quartets. Many believe this is the arrangement Robert Shaw employed. But according to Weston Noble, Mr. Shaw supported finding the best voices that would blend acoustically with one another using the procedure suggested in these pages or the procedure presented in *Achieving Choral Blend through Standing Position* (DVD, GIA). After arranging his bass section in a row, and each succeeding section in a row, he would then stand them on the choral risers in the following fashion. If there were eight basses, he would first find the best horizontal placement of the voices in each section.

```
8    7    6    5    4    3    2    1
◄------------------------------------------------
```

He would then arrange them on the risers vertically (not horizontally as is commonly believed) so that the resultant standing would be:

B1	S1	T1	A1	B5	S5	T5	A5
B2	S2	T2	A2	B6	S6	T6	A6
B3	S3	T3	A3	B7	S7	T7	A7
B4	S4	T4	A4	B8	S8	T8	A8

Conductor

Visually, without any previous knowledge of a specific standing procedure, one would assume this arrangement represents a "scattered quartet." In reality, it was the wish of Mr. Shaw to have the line arranged in such a vertical fashion.

Rather than quartet standings, the author finds it more desirable to use the seating arrangement that is presented below: "alto in the front" arrangement.

Curved Seating Arrangements

No matter what seating arrangement is used, it is crucial that the arrangement is severely curved in the shape of a "U." Such an arrangement maximizes hearing within the ensemble.

When a more straight or flat arrangement is used, two problems will be evident. First, the singers will find it more difficult to hear each other, and consequently, intonation will suffer. Second, choirs that sit in a more horizontal fashion will find it difficult, if not impossible, to achieve a "blended" sound. A choir sitting in such a horizontal arrangement will send the sound in the rehearsal room or concert hall directly into the hall. If any "mixing" of the sound is to occur, the choir is beholden to the acoustic of the room. However, if the choir sings in a sharply curved formation, where the outsides of the choir are almost facing each other, a mixing of the sound will take place before it enters the hall! Orchestras rehearse and play in a curved formation for that reason. Have you ever seen a large symphony orchestra sit horizontally, similar to the way a choir stands on "choral" risers?

"Alto in the Front" Seating Arrangement

Five years ago, I "rediscovered" this seating arrangement and have never returned to a traditional "block" arrangement of both rehearsing and concertizing. Weston Noble introduced me to this concept of choral seating. Consider the seating arrangement shown below for an SATB choir, using a **curved** formation. The singers marked in boldface type represent the beginning of the section as determined when an acoustical standing is done (as detailed in the following section).

Both arrangements are remarkably effective. Your acoustic surroundings and the ability of your singers will determine which is best. Weston Noble prefers the arrangement where the basses are in the third row because it places bass sound immediately behind the soprano sound and ensures better tuning. Mr. Noble has also stated that one of the reasons he believes this works incredibly well is that in addition to the altos being able to hear much better, their presence at the front of the choir acts as a "scrim" for the soprano sound, almost like an acoustic filter that takes the "edge" off of the soprano sound.

◀ -- ▶

T1	T1	T1	T1	T1	**T1**	**T2**	T2	T2	T2	T2	T2
B1	B1	B1	B1	B1	**B1**	**B2**	B2	B2	B2	B2	B2
S1	S1	S1	S1	S1	**S1**	**S2**	S2	S2	S2	S2	S2
A1	A1	A1	A1	A1	**A1**	**A2**	A2	A2	A2	A2	A2

Conductor

or

◄--►

B1	B1	B1	B1	B1	**B1**	**B2**	B2	B2	B2	B2	B2
T1	T1	T1	T1	T1	**T1**	**T2**	T2	T2	T2	T2	T2
S1	S1	S1	S1	S1	**S1**	**S2**	S2	S2	S2	S2	S2
A1	A1	A1	A1	A1	**A1**	**A2**	A2	A2	A2	A2	A2

Conductor

Adaptation of the Modified Seating Arrangement for Treble Choirs

The overriding principle with the "alto in the front" seating arrangement is that the alto section is at the front of the ensemble. This same principle can be applied to treble choirs. While the acoustic of the rehearsal or performance space will influence the placement of the other parts, the alto section should always be in front. For most situations, the first soprano should occupy the middle row, and the second soprano should occupy the back row. Beginning singers for each section determined by the acoustical standing procedure that follows are indicated in boldface type.

S1 S1 S1 S1 S1 S1 S1 S1 **S1**
S2 S2 S2 S2 S2 S2 S2 S2 **S2**
A1 A1 A1 A1 A1 **A1 A2** A2 A2 A2 A2 A2

Conductor

Acoustic Standing Procedure for All Choirs

Overtones within a voice, which are the unique by-product of resonances, are the core of any vocal sound. Overtone series are as varied as individual fingerprints. The paradigm that follows attempts to explain the issue.

Each voice possesses its own unique overtone series, which defines its own special timbre. That overtone series can be likened to various types of combs. Some combs have larger teeth that are more widely spaced; others have teeth that are narrower and spaced closer together. A comb with wider-spaced teeth will "fit together" with a comb that has more narrowly spaced teeth. The goal is to get two combs that fit together with complimentary teeth. The teeth are representative of the overtones in each voice. You want singers sitting adjacent to each other whose overtone series is complimentary or interlocking. When this is accomplished, a natural blend is elicited from singers that does **not** require them to compromise their vocal technique and allows for the best intonation possible. Singers who are sitting next to unlikely acoustical matches will produce an aural manifestation that is either "too loud" or "out of tune," or both. Seated in an inferior acoustic position within a choir, there is little a singer can do without vocal damage to either "blend" or "fix" pitch. The only hope is for the conductor to be highly skilled in deciding the optimal acoustic seating for the choir.

Following are the steps you should follow to accomplish an acoustically maximized seating arrangement for the choir:

1. The first time this is done, explain the principles to the choir and have the rest of the choir watch and listen to the proceeding.

2. Seat each section individually. That is, seat the alto 1 section separately from the alto 2 section.

3. Select the **beginning singer** for each section. The position for each of these singers in each section is indicated in boldface type in the diagrams above. The beginning singer can, in fact, be any singer in the section. If the conductor desires a brighter or a taller, narrower sound, then that voice type should be chosen. If a rounder or darker color is desired, then the section should begin with that voice type. To determine which singer that should be, have each singer sing in solo the first phrase of *My Country 'Tis of Thee*. (Other vocalises can be used; however, that one is most "honest" because it contains many dictional problems. If singers can sing in tune with each other on a more complex dictional challenge, then it ensures better success of the standing arrangement.) The keys listed below should be used for this procedure. Have each singer sing at a *piu forte* volume. These keys place the singers in the "middling" portions of their voices. In addition, they require singers to sing over their "lifts" or "breaks." Consequently, weaknesses of each voice are immediately exposed so as not to wreak havoc upon the standing arrangement when literature is employed.

A-flat:	First soprano
G-flat:	Second soprano
D-flat:	First alto
B-flat:	Second alto
G:	First tenor
G-flat:	Second tenor
D-flat:	Baritone
B-flat:	Bass

4. After the beginning singer has been selected for the section, then you need to determine the singer who will stand in the next position next to the beginning singer. The direction in which the line is built is dependent upon the choral arrangement that is to be used. For example, if you were using the set-up with alto voices in the front row, then the soprano 1 section should be built to the **right** of the beginning singer. In the same SATB arrangement, if you were seating the alto 2 section, then you would seat them to the left of the beginning singer. **Build each section in a straight line.**

5. Hear each singer sing in combination with the beginning singer. The rules for choosing the best acoustical match for each succeeding singer are as follows:

   - **Have singers sing *piu forte*. They should not attempt to "blend" with the singer next to them.** Singers must be encouraged to sing with a healthy, supported, free, and vibrant sound—the sound that is **their** sound. As will be repeated in the step that follows, be aware of the "friend factor" (the desire to blend with a friend when near that person in the line). In most cases, singers will under-sing to accomplish this, thus giving an inaccurate result in the standing procedure.

   - **Tell singers to listen but make no attempt to blend.** Be aware of the "friend factor." Many times, singers who are singing next to a friend will make an attempt to blend by either under-singing or possibly singing off the breath. Be attentive for this, and constantly emphasize that while the singers should listen to everyone else except themselves, they should not attempt to blend into the sectional sound.

Permit singers, however, to close the vowel (i.e., wrap their lips around the sound) in an attempt to "fit into" the sectional sound.

- **Avoid singers who seem to cause rhythmic "sluggishness."** Some singers, when tried in various positions within the line, seem to cause the rhythm to become sluggish or lethargic. Do not allow these singers to sing in that position, regardless of whether they sing in tune. Over a period of time, that rhythmic "laziness" will carry over into the sectional sound and cause intonation problems within the section. Allow only those singers who enhance or create a rhythmically vital and alive sound.

- **Select the singer who sings best in tune with the rest of the line.** If there are several singers who sing in tune with the beginning singer, choose the one who is most in tune. If there are several who sing in tune, then and only then can you make a decision based upon the color of the sound.

Note: Many people believe you should place the singers with "better ears" near the center of the ensemble to produce the "pitch core" of the choir. This should not be done for many reasons. Applying the procedure that is being outlined, stronger singers will be placed naturally throughout the ensemble. Also, weaker singers will end up in position between two stronger singers. If stronger ears are placed at the center of the ensemble, this will actually weaken the pitch stability of the entire ensemble.

6. When the next voice has been determined, then have those two voices sing with each remaining singer in the section. To arrive at the next singer, repeat the procedure above. Select the singer who sings best in tune with the two singers already chosen. Proceed singer by singer until all the singers have been placed.

7. **When you have stood the entire section, place the singer who is in the final position in the beginning singer position.** The beginning singer you chose would then occupy the second place in the line. When you try this, you will often find that the sound of the entire line will improve dramatically. If it does, then that is the final standing for the line. If the composite sound is worse, then return the singer to the final position at the end of the line. Number the line consecutively

starting with the beginning singer. For example, if you are numbering the soprano 1 section, the numbers would be as follows:

Remember that boldface type indicates the **beginning singer.**

(section built to the left)

◀--

S1	S1	S1	S1	S1	S1	S1	S1	S1	S1	S1	S1	S1	S1	**S1**
15	14	13	12	11	10	9	8	7	6	5	4	3	2	1

8. No matter the arrangement used, the **numerical** order must be kept in tact when placing singers on choral risers. If it is not possible to keep the entire section in a single row, then the numeric order can be broken, but it must come into center each time the line is broken. For example, if the section has to be placed in two rows:

◀--

15	14	13	12	11	10	9	8
7	6	5	4	3	2	1	

◀--

If the section needs to be divided into three rows:

15	14	13	12	11

◀--

10	9	8	7	6

◀--

5	4	3	2	1

Never use the numbers in these alternating directions:

11	12	13	14	15

◀--

6	7	8	9	10

--▶

5	4	3	2	1

◀--

You can split the section in as many rows as needed as long as you always come back to center!

Remember that the position of the beginning voice determines the direction in which the row is stood on the risers! As an example, if you were seating Alto 2 using the arrangement with alto in the front row, then your line would be as follows:

(built to the singers' **left**)

---▶

A2 A2 A2 A2 A2 A2 A2 A2 A2
1   2   3   4   5   6   7   8   9

Turning Order Inside Out to Change Sound

Once the standing has been completed, if you turn the row inside out, the result will be the opposite color the row had before reversal. For example, if the final row is numbered:

1   2   3   4   5   6   7

The inside out order would be:

7   6   5   4   3   2   1

With younger or inexperienced choirs, it is possible to change the tone color of the choir by reversing the rows in this manner. For example, if a standing is done with a Renaissance tone color in mind, then reversing the row will most likely produce a darker tone color suitable for romantic music.

A Word of Caution:

When standing next to taller singers, shorter singers will not be able to sing in tune regardless of their music aptitude. The reason is that the sound is above them, so they cannot hear it accurately to sing in tune. The only solution for shorter singers is to have them stand on boxes that will put them at an equal level with taller singers. The opposite is also true. Taller singers will need to stand on a lower step of the choral riser if they are to sing in tune. Left unattended, both shorter and taller singers will not be able to "blend" into the composite choral sound.

Acoustical Auditions for Highly Select Ensembles

In addition to using musical criterion to choose voices for select ensembles, award final placement within the ensemble only after an acoustical standing procedure is done. This means no singer should be awarded a place in the final roster of the ensemble unless each voice can be acoustically stood within the ensemble. This not only ensures that the final choices for the ensemble can sing in tune, but it also implies that even larger voices will "blend" without sacrificing their vocal technique.

Seating Arrangement for Large SATB Choirs

The advantage of the set-up shown below is twofold. First, it allows for men to be grouped together. And second, the pitch centers of the choir, the outer parts, are placed adjacent to each other: S1, B2, T1.

```
S1 S1 S1 S1 B2 B2 B2 B2 T1 T1 T1 T1 A2 A2 A2 A2
S1 S1 S1 S1 B2 B2 B2 B2 T1 T1 T1 T1 A2 A2 A2 A2
S2 S2 S2 S2 B1 B1 B1 B1 T2 T2 T2 T2 A1 A1 A1 A1
S2 S2 S2 S2 B1 B1 B1 B1 T2 T2 T2 T2 A1 A1 A1 A1
```
Conductor

Seating Arrangement for Choirs with Fewer Men

Conductors are encouraged to "experiment" with standing arrangements for choirs with less-than-balanced voicings. Do not be afraid to break out of the box and try something out of the ordinary. Just remember that the rule of thumb should always be to choose a standing arrangement that will **sound** the best.

When dealing with the acoustics of a room, choose the standing arrangement that will maximize the sound of the choir. As a rule of thumb, place men's voices in the center of the set-up, and surround those voices with the female voices. Also remember to curve the set-up as much as possible! The bold-faced voice parts below signify placement of for the beginning voice of the part.

```
S1 S1 S1 S1 S1 S1
S1 S1 S1 B2 B2 B2 S1 S1 S1
S2 S2 S2 T1 T1 T1 S2 S2 S2
A1 A1 A1 T2 T2 A2 A2 A2
       Conductor
```

Transferring Seating Arrangements from Rehearsal Space to Concert Space

Many times an acoustic standing arrangement is sabotaged when transferred to standing choral risers or chancel set-up using existing seating. The rule of thumb should always be to take the seating arrangement you decided upon and re-mold it to resemble as close as possible an open-ended box with sharp corners. The reason for this is simple. Such an arrangement allows for the set-up to "mix" the sound before it goes into the hall rather than the hall mixing the choir's sound for you. Be less concerned with the "look" of the choir and more concerned with how they sound. Also experiment with placement on the stage or chancel. Try the arrangement near the back wall, then try it more forward, and choose the one that sounds best. Such arrangements with choral risers will require you to place the risers at right angles, which will expose holes at the right angles. The arrangement shown below:

```
B1 B1 B1 B1 B1 B1 B2 B2 B2 B2 B2 B2
T1 T1 T1 T1 T1 T1 T2 T2 T2 T2 T2 T2
S1 S1 S1 S1 S1 S1 S2 S2 S2 S2 S2 S2
A1 A1 A1 A1 A1 A1 A2 A2 A2 A2 A2 A2
            Conductor
```

becomes this arrangement in concert:

```
B1 B1 B2 B2 B2
T1 T1 T2 T2 T2
S1 S1 S1 S2 S2 S2
   A1 A1 A2
```

B1 T1 S1 A1   *A2 S2 T2 B2*
B1 T1 S1 A1   *A2 S2 T2 T2 B2*
B1 T1 S1 A1   *A2 S2 T2 B2*
B1 T1 S1 A1   *A2 S2 T2 B2*

Notice the placement of the beginning voices in this arrangement. The numeric order, then, would proceed from the beginning voice outward in each section. Voice parts in italics face inward, or turn on a 45-degree angle **inward** during concert. The piano, if used, should be placed in the center of the choir.

Chapter 14

Energizing the Sound of the Choir: A Philosophical Challenge

> So Socrates was mistaken: it's not the unexamined life that is not worth living; it's the uncommitted life. There is no smaller package in the world than that of a person all wrapped up in himself. Love is our business. (p. 12)
>
> William Sloane Coffin
> *The Heart Is a Little to the Left*

While vocal technique provides a formidable challenge to any conductor, energizing the sound of the choir through extra-musical means is, perhaps, the biggest challenge on a day-to-day basis. Despite one's mastery of the instructional aspects of teaching vocal technique to a choir, those of us who have dealt with choirs will attest to the fact that regardless of the diligence over proper singing technique, many times the sound of the choir lacks brilliance, resonance, and a certain unmistakable clarity. Dull, cloudy, and out-of-tune sounds sometimes are the result of our work.

Most of us instinctively begin to work harder and elicit more energy from ourselves in the desperate hope that our energy will transfer and vitalize the dead sound within the ensemble. Many times this works, but many times it does not. One of the many symptoms of this lackluster, dull sound is that the community of the choir breeds a lack of personal commitment in producing one's sound. Personal responsibility is less accountable in this group situation. And, unfortunately, the larger the choir, the less individual accountability there seems to be. While it is important for the conductor to always be an alive, energetic, and communicative human being, the responsibility for sound and the quality of that sound must fall on the individual singers.

I often say the best rehearsal technique is that technique which skillfully places **all** responsibility upon the singers, leaving the conductor the tasks of breathing, listening, reacting, and evoking sounds. To accomplish that end, one must make a major philosophical adjustment in the way one warms up the choir and be armed with an arsenal of techniques that will continually place the responsibility for alive and vital sound upon the individual singers.

To do this, remember that warming up a choir is similar to a pedagogical seesaw. On one side of the seesaw are all of the vocal techniques that have been presented in this book. On the other side of the seesaw are all of the techniques that can cause singers to be constantly reminded of their responsibility to bring alive singing to the rehearsal. The choices made concerning how to teach the choir to hear represent the fulcrum of the seesaw. All must be kept in mind when teaching the choir during the choral warm-up process.

The various approaches are numbered to help organize your thought process. Understand that the numbering does not imply a hierarchical importance to these points. On any given day, several of the points may be in issue. On the worst rehearsal days, all of the points may need to be addressed in some way.

Approach 1: The Dulling World of Our Daily Lives

One of the most difficult obstacles facing any choral warm-up is that the choir enters the rehearsal or performance after part or all of a day of numbing external influences in the world. These influences, many and varied depending on our life situation, tend to cause us to "blend" and, in many cases, contribute to a state that may described as dull or less alive. These influences cause us to deaden gradually over the course of the day. They chip away slowly at our human aliveness and vitality.

The first step toward correction is acknowledging this obstacle. Understanding what it is to be an alive human being is central to a pedagogical solution. I know several persons who preach this to the choir but are unable to model this state of existence honestly. They tend to act alive, but really aren't. The result is a driven and agitated sound that is harsh and full of intonation problems. A certain awareness that the world is doing this to us, as well as inspiring words compelling and empowering singers into a more alive state, is at the core of this keystone of both the warm-up and the rehearsal. Calling people into an alive condition is possible and, at times, can even be inspiring. Dullness and complacency must not be allowed in the rehearsal room. Singers must understand that once identified, it is their responsibility to enliven and inspirit themselves.

Approach 2: Awareness

Choral sound will never be exciting, vital, and in tune unless the singers are in constant state of **total** awareness. This state of awareness is primarily an awareness of their bodies—all of their bodies all of the time! This is difficult because few persons, if any, are in this state of awareness throughout their day. We tend to carry ourselves through our daily routine relatively numb to our bodies and ourselves. Simple verbal associative cues can remind and call singers into a state of higher body awareness. Remember that when one sings in a group, responsibility for one's awareness reduces at a dramatic rate.

Awareness can be stimulated through carefully chosen verbiage interspersed through the warm-up process. Phrases such as the following are usually sufficient to call singers into a higher state of awareness:

- Are you aware of your whole body when singing?
- Are you aware of your back?
- Are you aware of the space that surrounds your body?
- Sing with your whole body.
- Are you aware of every square inch of skin on your body when you sing?
- Can you give more energy?
- Can you stay aware for the whole rehearsal?
- Imagine a situation or experience in your life when you have been in an aware state.

Approach 3: Bringing a Rhythmic Commitment to the Singing Process

Commitment to one's vocal sound is difficult to describe. In its most broad terms, commitment refers to a total desire to sing and sing well. This is difficult to achieve because so much of life and life experiences require the opposite: a lessening of individual commitment. While one can "talk" about commitment, explanations always or most always fall short. A physical representation of commitment is the most efficient pedagogical tool available.

At several points in this book, pointing has been used to correct many vocal issues. But it is important to teach the experience of commitment through one's singing and being. By pointing on every note that is sung, one brings a commitment to the exact attack of the pitch, almost unknowingly.

Pointing also teaches singers to trust their instincts. Pointing is a physical technique to teach the importance of self-trust and the importance of singing now without hesitation. Commitment to sound can be interpreted as the ability to sing within the "now," without hesitation. The promise to sing each note without hesitation and with the same belief that binds our lives together with the things we most believe is the same promise that is brought to sound through pointing.

Pointing with energy and aliveness will immediately vitalize choral sound. Just as you point emphatically when punctuating what you believe in spoken word, you can also "punctuate" sound with a physical commitment embodied in pointing. By focusing on pointing, you can draw singers toward a higher state of commitment—a feeling, an awareness. Commitment brings with it aliveness and an unmistakable energy. Singers will quickly enjoy the benefits of this state of commitment and will begin to yearn for it in every rehearsal. When this is achieved, choral sound is always alive, vital, resonant, and in tune.

Approach 4: Causing Singers to Understand the Miracle of Awe and Wonder

> The purpose of art is not the release of a momentary ejection of adrenalin but is, rather, the gradual, lifelong construction of a state of wonder and serenity.
>
> Glenn Gould
> Interview for *Musical America*, 1962

For music to exist in an honest and exciting art form, regardless of the age of the singers, a fantasy must be present in the rehearsal room. Fantasy is the stuff of musical creation. Without "fantasy," music is dull and despondent. It brings nothing to uplift the human condition let alone vocal sound. Fantasy that allows singers to constantly be in a state of awe and wonder is central to the production of expressive vocal tone.

Awe and wonder are decidedly lacking in the world in which we live. Great art, whether written, sounded, painted, sculpted, or photographed, constantly provides insight into the true nature of awe and wonder. A certain innocence is a central ingredient for awe and wonder. It is also a central ingredient to any discovery process. Prior life experiences are, perhaps, the most expedient entrances into the world of awe and wonder.

I can remember my first visit to Chartres Cathedral in France. After studying the stained glass of that cathedral and looking at many photographs, there was nothing that could prepare me to walk into that space. Becoming awash in such a blue beauty placed me in a wordless state. I cannot describe awe and wonder, but I can assure you I felt it. In fact, I was overcome by it. I was overcome with awe and wonder at the birth of my daughter. There are few things as awe-inspiring as the beginning of a life. Holding her in my arms in her first moments of life defies description but can begin to define awe and wonder. The true feeling of awe and wonder overcomes all of one's senses.

Another characteristic of awe and wonder is that it always occurs in serendipity with love—love of color, love of sound, and love of life and living. Awe and wonder cannot be present in any rehearsal room without love and care. Awe and wonder surrounds love and being loved. One cannot act awe and wonder; one needs to live and relive awe and wonder on a minute-by-minute basis. When one sings, it must always come from a place of awe and wonder.

Awe and wonder are the only true vehicles for music making. Great music, by its very composition, is infused with awe and wonder. But its sonic beauty will never be realized unless the choir sings through the door of awe and wonder. Arrival into and at the state of aesthetic fantasy, and ultimately a heightened state of aesthetic reality, should be one of the overriding and compelling objectives of any warm-up or rehearsal. Sound is the by-product of awe and wonder.

PART VI

PHYSICAL GESTURE AND KINESTHETIC AS TEACHING TOOLS

Chapter 15
Physical Gestures to Reinforce Choral Warm-Up Principles

Throughout this text, there has been a pedagogical case made for the use of gesture to reinforce proper singing principles within a choral ensemble. The gestural "vocabulary" that is listed below is made as a suggestion. Gestures can be combined or modified, and applied to portions or entire **Core Vocal Exercises** as the conductor deems necessary. Remember that the primary role of these gestures is to ensure that the singers are employing proper aspects of vocal technique within a group setting. In fact, the use of these gestures will ensure particular elements of vocal technique are being employed.

Pointing

Pointing is one of the most useful gestures that can serve one or many pedagogical purposes in the rehearsal. Possible uses of pointing are as follows:

- To clarify the attack of each note and to minimize or eliminate glissando or portamento that causes inaccurate pitch in the choir.
- To energize a sound, which leads to energized choral sound.
- To place responsibility for attack and rhythmic exactness upon each singer.
- To infuse energy into a lackluster choral sound.
- When performed in the right region, to bring more head tone into the choral sound.
- To provide a tactile symbolization of spiritual commitment brought to the production of sounds.

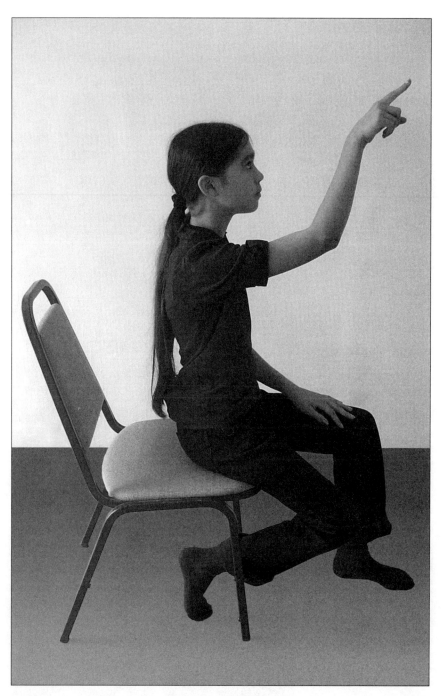

Figure 21 Pointing Gesture (notice the correct location of the point of the finger and its direction)

Up and Over

This gesture is used to subconsciously reinforce the concept of making space for sound and maintaining that sound in a high and forward position. This gesture can also suggest a lengthening of the spine and a release of the A/O joint as sound is being produced.

Figure 22 Up and Over

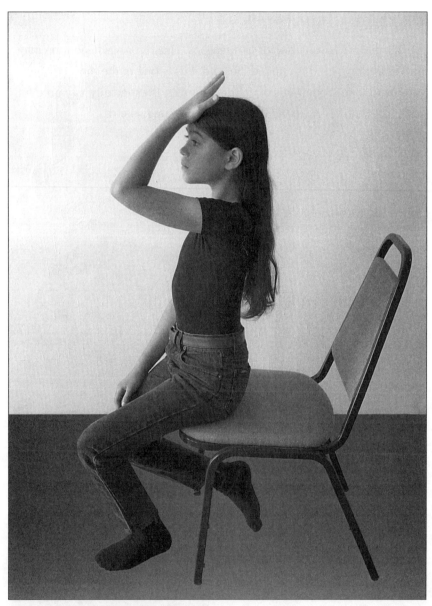

Figure 23 Heel of Hand on Forehead

Heel of Hand on Forehead

One of the most difficult pedagogical challenges, yet one of the most helpful for improving choral sound, is to make certain the sound produced by singers is **always** high and forward. By placing the heel of the hand on the forehead, singers will subconsciously always "place" sound in a higher, more forward position.

Finger Toss into Forehead

This gesture is valuable for two reasons. First, it brings head tone into any sound to which it is applied. Second, this is one of the most efficient gestures to take weight out of choral sound. It is especially valuable for music that requires rhythmic buoyancy in the sung sound.

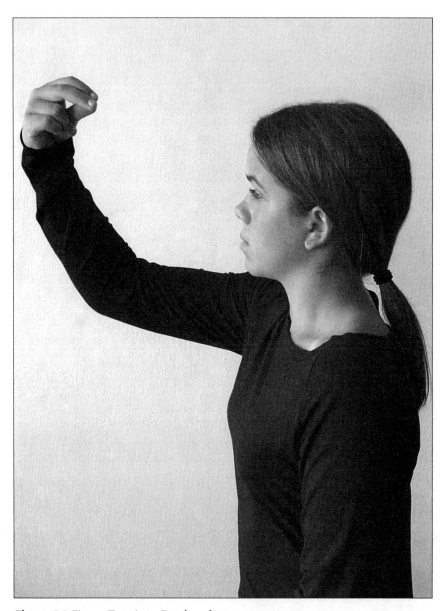

Figure 24 Finger Toss into Forehead

Toss Open Leg Lift

This gesture is invaluable for range extension exercises. When the leg is lifted and the arms are simultaneously opened, it takes the singer's mind off of the vocal mechanism so the voice can execute the technique required.

Figure 25 Toss Open Leg Lift

Figure 26 Forward Spin

Forward Spin

This technique greatly assists conductors to teach the concept of the constant and forward movement of air that is crucial to good singing. The gesture not only relays the kinesthetic of forward-moving air, but it also represents the energy that must be contained in the forward movement of the air.

Breath "Kneading" Gesture

This is one of the most effective gestures I have found to teach the complex act described as "support." In one gesture, choir members are taught the feeling of "on the breath" and supported sound around an alignment core and low center of breath.

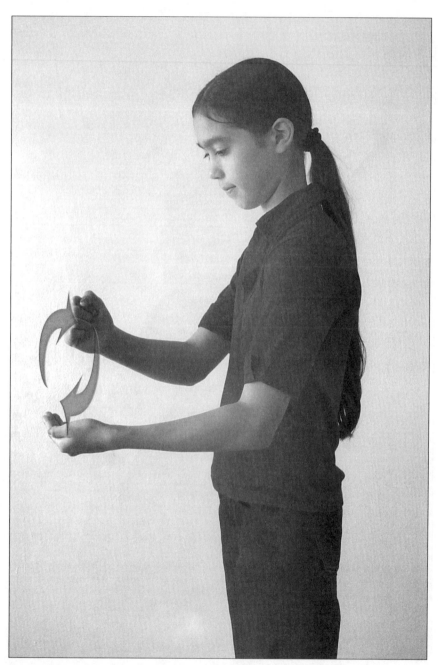

Figure 27 Breath "Kneading" Gesture

Forward Ball Toss

This gesture is most useful when applied to range extension exercises. The throwing gesture reinforces not only the energy required to sing a leap, but it also reinforces the concept of an increase in space for all singing that is in the upper register or that leaps into the upper register.

Figure 28 Forward Ball Toss

Dipping

This movement assists range extension exercises. The body moves downward as sound ascends, which helps to keep support low in the body.

Figure 29 Dipping

Body Tip

Tipping the head, especially for male voices, helps to maintain space in the upper register and assists in closing the vowel. These two techniques in combination are often referred to as "covering" in vocal pedagogy literature.

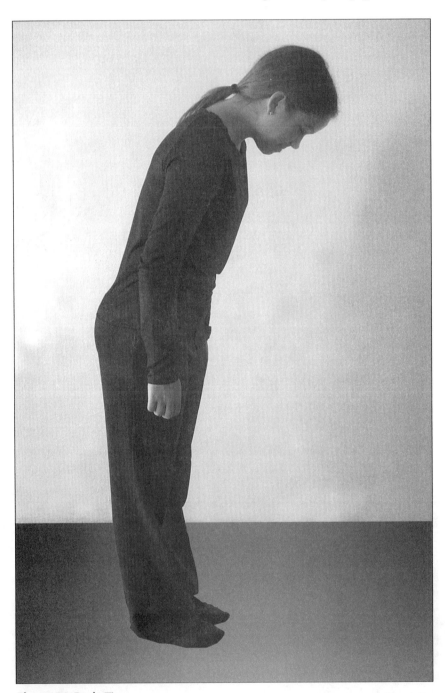

Figure 30 Body Tip

Breath Anchor and Space Umbrella Diagonal

These two gestures should be done concurrently for maximum pedagogical effect. The left hand formed into a fist symbolizes the exact location or kinesthetic sensation of breath placement within the core of the body. The hand over the head represents the space that is also needed in all well-produced vocal sound. Notice that there is a straight but **diagonal** line formed between the left-handed fist and the right-handed umbrella over the back of the head. (See Figure 31.)

Flick and Lighten (Tip of the Tongue "L" Finger Flick)

This gesture is most valuable when faster, lighter, and more quickly executed consonants are desired. Performed in the area of the forehead, it can also serve to bring more head tone into the sound. The gesture is most effective when teaching American choirs how to quickly articulate the tip of the tongue "L." (See Figure 32.)

Finger Twirl Over the Head

This spinning gesture directly over the crown of the head accomplishes several objectives. First, it infuses head tone into the sound. Second, it teaches the choir how to "spin," or allow the sound to be energized in a forward-moving fashion. (See Figure 33.)

Drooping Hands

As singers descend into their lower register, the sound often becomes "tight" because the vocal mechanism is "held" or possibly begins to rise. This gesture infuses an immediate freedom into all tight and held sounds. (See Figure 34.)

Resonance Swimming Cap Peel

For choral sounds that require maximum resonential output on the part of the singers, maximum use must be made of **all** resonances possible. An efficient and easy way to maximize the resonance capability of the singers is to use the analogy of a person taking a swimming cap slowly off the head and then filling the head area exposed by the removed cap. (See Figure 35.)

Figure 31 Breath Anchor and Space Umbrella Diagonal

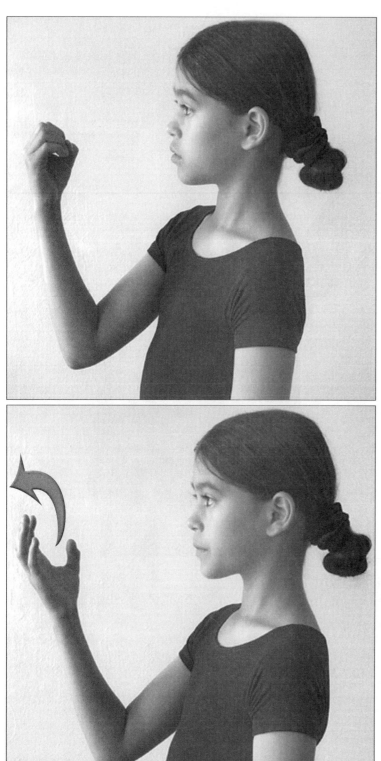

Figure 32 Flick and Lighten (Tip of the Tongue "L" Finger Flick)

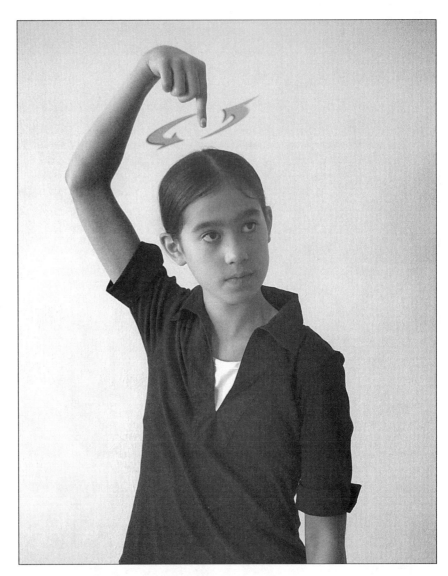

Figure 33 Finger Twirl Over the Head

Figure 34 Drooping Hands

Figure 35 Resonance Swimming Cap Peel

High and Forward Finger Wand (the "oo" Magnet)

The "oo" vowel is problematic because American singers tend to produce the vowel with too backward a placement (i.e., a "jowel" vowel). By singing the "oo" vowel into the finger held at eye level and forward of the face, the vowel is "teased" into a higher and more forward position.

Figure 36 High and Forward Finger Wand (the "oo" Magnet)

Tossing Clap

This is a valuable gesture adapted from Dalcroze that allows choirs to kinesthetically understand the weight that is required for any style of music. The key to this gesture is to make certain the clap is thrown from side to side, across the midline of the body. The weight of the clap can be varied infinitely to represent the desired stylistic weight to be "felt" in the sung sound. The gesture is effective for both adding weight and taking away weight in all styles of choral music.

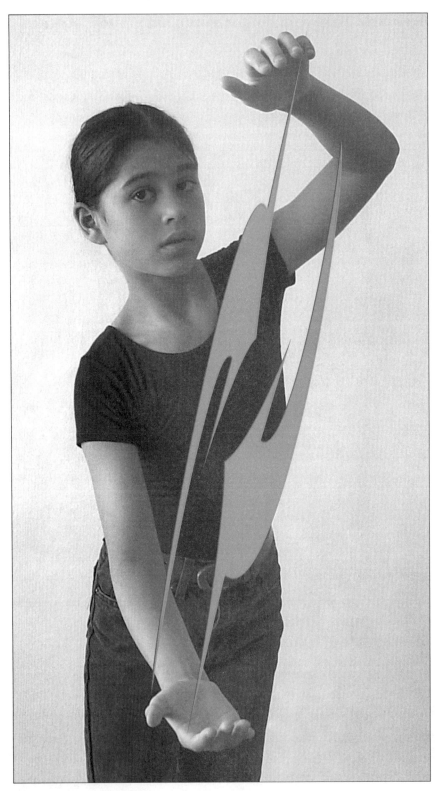

Figure 37 Tossing Clap

Hand Dab for Energy

Many times it is difficult to relay to a choir how to "energize" a dull sound. Many times, adding a simple "hand dab" will energize the sound. A direct, energetic motion that does not lock on its rebound will accomplish that purpose.

Figure 38 Hand Dab for Energy

Hand Smoothing Gesture

Many times the concept of legato, or the maintenance of legato, is difficult for choirs to maintain. Again, the use of a hand gesture coupled with an appropriate vocalise can accomplish this. The gesture should be a smooth and continuous motion from left to right. The hand could be held parallel to the floor, but there may be an inherent danger that the resulting sound would be overly dark and unspacious. A better hand position would be one similar to the use of the hand when to mix water and soap together in a bath. The gesture should be done with only one hand. (See Figures 39–40.)

Figure 39 Hand Smoothing Gesture (Left to Right) – Beginning Position

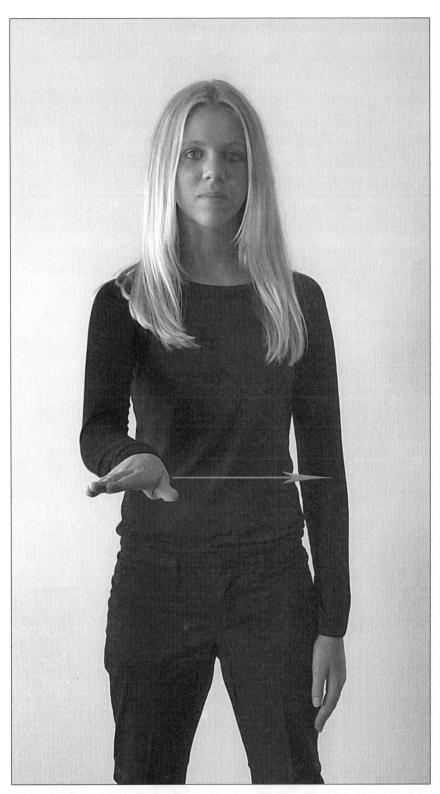

Figure 40 Hand Smoothing Gesture (Left to Right)—"Outside" Position

Congealing Sound Mixing Gesture

At times it may difficult for a choir to understand how to "mix" various aspects of vocal technique into an appropriately healthy and free vocal sound. Marrying the concepts of vertical spaciousness and high and forward vocal placement is especially difficult. This can be accomplished fairly simply by using the following gesture.

Begin the gesture as an overhead umbrella, similar to the one employed for space in the sigh. Bring the hands over the head, and then move them together toward a point that is about a 45-degree angle. Have the singers stop the forward movement when they hear a good sound—that is, when the sound is most clear and beautiful. Over-extension of the hands will result in a sound that is overly bright. Stopping prematurely will produce a sound that is placed in the rear of the mouth and spread. (See Figures 41–44.)

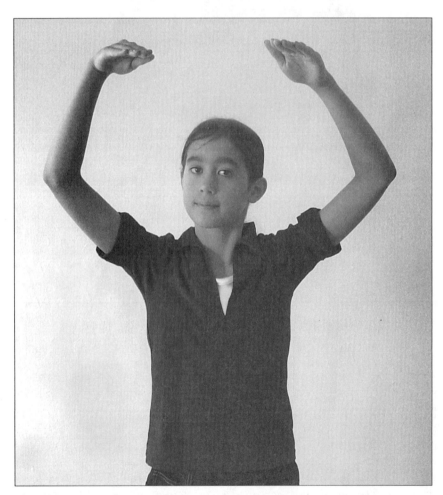

Figure 41 Congealing Sound Mixing Gesture – Beginning Position

Figure 42 Congealing Sound Mixing Gesture – Middle Position

Figure 43 Congealing Sound Mixing Gesture – End Position

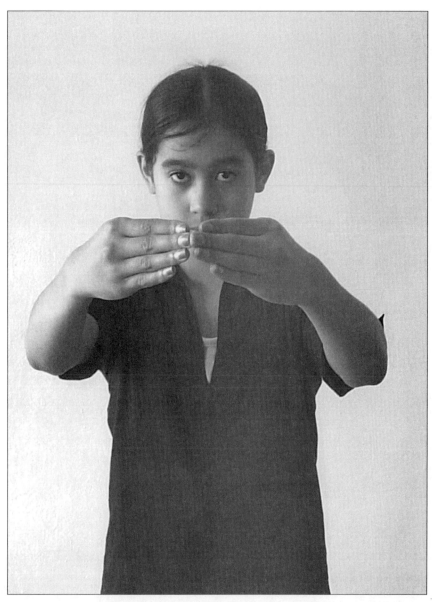

Figure 44 Congealing Sound Mixing Gesture – Undesirable End Position

165

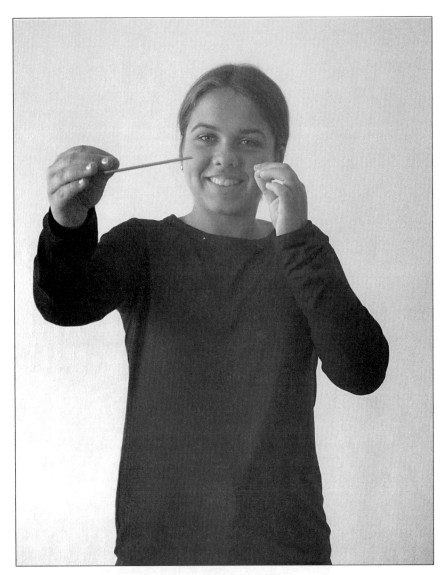

Figure 45 Linguine Pull Gesture – Front View

Linguine Pull Gesture

Choirs often have difficulty singing through vowel sounds and maintaining the forward "spin" in the sound. In addition, they have problems maintaining the high and forward placement for vowel sounds. This gesture not only accomplishes all those goals, but it also ensures constant forward movement of the sound(s) that are rhythmically vital. Care must be taken to ensure that the gesture is performed in a high and forward fashion.

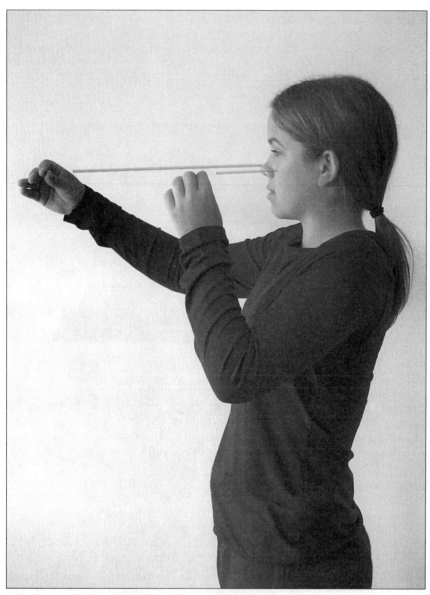

Figure 46 Linguine Pull Gesture – Side View

Upward Cheekbone Brush

This physical gesture is useful to reinforce high and forward placement. The heel of both hands should gently brush the cheekbones and move upward at a 45-degree angle.

Figure 47 Upward Cheekbone Brush – Beginning Position

Sound Rolling Gesture (for *piano* and *pianissimo* dynamics)

In addition to closing the vowel and maintaining vertical spaciousness to achieve a vibrant, in-tune *piano* or *pianissimo* sound, it is often helpful to instruct the choir to roll the sound forward in the face, maintaining a high and forward placement to the vowel. This will enable the singers to increase the *piano* dynamic toward *pp* or *ppp*.

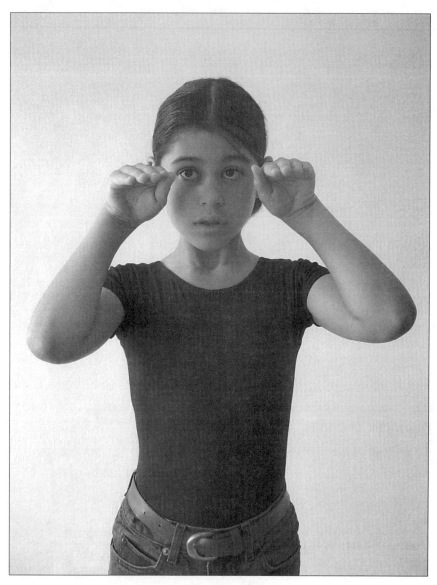

Figure 48 Sound Rolling Gesture – Beginning Position (for *piano* and *pianissimo* dynamics)

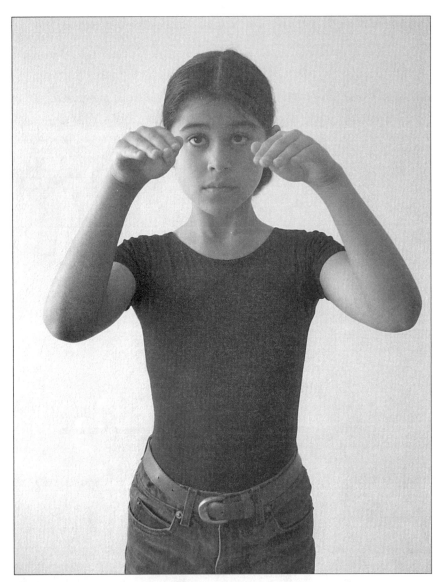

Figure 49 Sound Rolling Gesture – Ending Position
(for *piano* and *pianissimo* dynamics)

Consonant Wisp Gesture

In some situations, it is desirable to have light and "disappearing" endings to some phrases. This technique is especially useful when singing in French, where it is important for phrase endings to disappear with a vanishing sound.

Figure 50 Consonant Wisp Gesture—Beginning Position

Figure 51 Consonant Wisp Gesture – Ending Position

Upward Toss (for sound weight reduction)

Many times, choirs will carry too much vocal weight into the choral sound in pieces that require a more transparent texture, such as madrigals and music of the renaissance. This gesture is especially valuable for pieces that move at a fast tempo, where the consonant weight is both causing the pitch to go flat and slowing the forward movement of the musical line.

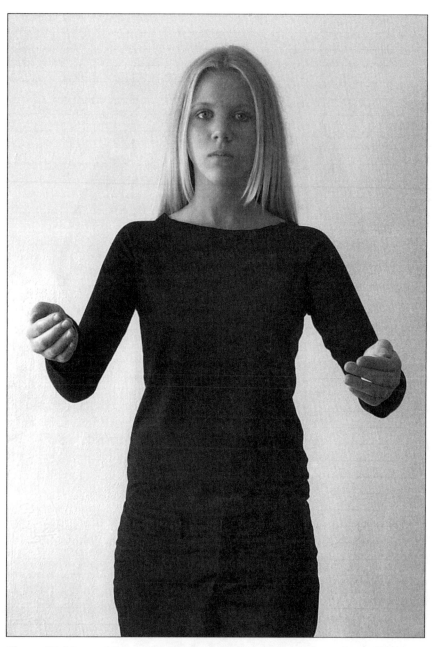

Figure 52 Upward Toss – Beginning Position (for sound weight reduction)

Figure 53 Upward Toss – Ending Position (for sound weight reduction)

Chapter 16
An Application of the Work of Rudolf von Laban to Propel Musical Line

Motion comes from emotion.

Children use kinesthesia to learn about their world. But Western education attempts to train the mind, and pays little attention to the kinesthetic sense.

Robert M. Abramson
Dalcroze Eurhythmics, video

While it has lately been popular in certain quarters to equate body movement with the "natural" and the "authentic" in human behavior, there is actually very little instinctive about the way we move. Due to the nature of the human brain, as mentioned earlier, voluntary movement must be learned through interaction with other human beings within a social context. Consequently, body movement is a highly structured, culturally coded form of symbolic communication, equivalent in its sophistication to the better-known extension systems of language, music, mathematics, and so on. As part of the extended world, human movement has become an abstraction of the real, biological world. Paradoxically, body movement is at once natural and contrived, visceral and symbolic, personal and social, ever present and constantly disappearing. (pp. 84–85)

Carol-Lynne Moore, Kaoru Yamamoto
Beyond Words

Looking at the whole range of innate and acquired impulses of man, one is tempted to search for a common denominator. In my opinion, this denominator is not mere motion, but movement with all its spiritual implication.... What has to be done today—and our time seems to stand on the threshold of a new awareness of movement—is to acknowledge movement as the great integrator. This involves, of course, the conviction that movement is the vehicle which concerns the whole man with all his physical and spiritual facilities. To be able to see this great unity is not the privilege of the artist alone. Everybody, every single individual, has this unity at the basis of his natural tendencies and impulses, which can be lifted out of the treasure of forgotten truth and cultivated in all the various ramifications of life. (pp. 12–13)

Rudolf von Laban
The Laban Art of Movement Guild Magazine

What one experiences through movement can never be expressed in words; in a simple step there may be a reverence of which we are scarcely aware. Yet through it something higher than just tenderness and devotion may flow into us and from us. (p. 35)

Rudolf von Laban
A Life for Dance

Of Laban's four words, weight probably is of special significance to rhythm. To perform a crusis with appropriate weight, one needs to prepare the crusis in audiation. A physical analogy may be helpful: just as there is a feeling for the shifting of weight involved in the preparation of a physical jump, so there is a feeling for the shifting of weight involved in the preparation of a crusis, that is, in the anacrusis. Unless one can jump (not hop), he will not be able to audiate or perform an anacrusis properly, because an anacrusis must incorporate the same feeling for crescendo (upward weight shift) that is characteristic of a jump. Moreover, without a feeling for relative weight and ability to shift weight at will, one will not be able to sustain movement appropriately, and without sustained movement there can be no feeling for space and flow. To engage properly in rigid (bound) sustained flow in performance, one must be audiating unbound sustained flow. (p. 155)

Edwin E. Gordon
Learning Sequences in Music, 1993

From its birth, music has registered the rhythms of the human body of which it is the complete and idealized sound image. It has been the basis of human emotion all down the ages. The successive transformations of musical rhythms, from century to century, correspond so closely to the transformations of character and temperament that, if a musical phrase of any typical composition is played, the entire mental state of the period at which was composed is revived; and, by association of ideas, there is aroused in our own bodies the muscular echo or response of the bodily movements imposed at the period in question by social conventions and necessities. If we would restore to the body all rhythms it has gradually forgotten, we must not only offer it as models the jolting, rioting rhythms of savage music, but also gradually initiate it into the successive transformations which time has given to these elementary rhythms. (p. 7)

Musical rhythmic movement consists of linking up durations, geometry consists of linking up fragments of space, while living plastic movement links up degrees of energy. (p. 10)

Economy and balance: such should be our motto. We must economize our nervous expenditure, which expresses itself in angry starts, sudden, irregular, impatient movements, depression, hypersensitiveness. We must economize our time, cease work before the point of fatigue is reached, anticipate the moment when rest becomes necessary. And we must economize our will to progress, moderate our appetites, and balance our desires of creation with the means at our command. (p. 12)

Emile Jaques-Dalcroze
Eurhythmics Art and Education

It goes without saying that a musical phrase is movement, and vice versa. As singers, our movements relay our innermost rhythm, musical line, and textural colors. At times, our movement courts the singers to move their sound in response to our gesture, and at other times, our conducting mimes the sound that is in our inner musical fantasy world. The ability to move freely is a prerequisite for the study and understanding of music phrasing. The ability to reacquaint oneself with the infinite vocabulary of movement is an essential readiness for music making. The body must be reacquainted with its full movement potential so that through movement, one can elicit, evoke, excite, awaken, mirror, court, and reflect the sound of each piece.

As children, each one of us experienced the **entire** world of movement. In our play we ran, we jumped, we swung. We leaped and rolled and tumbled, skipped and hopped. We moved by ourselves and with others. We played circle games. Play was movement. Serious play was on the playground and in the home. Life was play, and play was movement. Movement was our lives. As we grew older and more mature, we began to move less and less. Play became a less prominent part of our life. Movement no longer felt natural and spontaneous. As our bodies grew, we moved less and less. The world we grew into did not encourage movement. Consequently, as we grew older, we settled upon a limited, yet efficient movement vocabulary that would get us through our day-to-day life. Can that spontaneous movement of early childhood be rediscovered? Yes! Is that rediscovered movement world necessary for the development of the beginning conductor? Yes. The work of Rudolf von Laban can reawaken life movement experiences so they can be used in singing.

Rudolf von Laban

Rudolf von Laban was born in 1879 in Bratislava, Hungary, the son of an army general. His early years were preoccupied with observing movement. As a child, he spent considerable time drawing and visualizing patterns in space. His desire to understand both physical and mental effort led him to a lengthy course of study in painting, sculpture, and stage design in Paris, Berlin, and Vienna. As part of his training, he studied various cultures, particularly the natives of Africa, the people of the Near East, and the Chinese.

In 1910, Laban founded his first dance group and school in Munich, where he developed one of his favorite genres: the movement choir. During World War I, he lived in Switzerland and continued to develop his ideas. In 1919, he formed a stage dance group, the Tanzbuhne Laban, which specialized in expressive dance. Through that ensemble, he created many full-length dance compositions (*The Swinging Cathedral, Die Geblendeten, Gaukelei, Don Juan,* and *Die Nacht*).

In 1926, Laban founded the Choreographic Institute in Wurzburg, which he later moved to Berlin. That institute specialized in the development of a dance notation system, originally known as *Eukinetics,* which was published in 1928 as *Kinetography.* In the United States, his work is known as *Labanotation.*

Laban became director of movement at the Berlin State Opera in 1930 and subsequently was recognized as one of Europe's most famous choreographers.

Unable to continue work under the Nazi regime, Laban and some of his pupils sought sanctuary in the United Kingdom. Laban introduced modern educational dance into the schools as a new creative subject. In Manchester, England, where he lived from 1942 to 1953, he helped establish the Art of Movement Studio with Lisa Ullman. Concurrently, he established the Laban-Lawrence Industrial Rhythm, which developed new approaches for the selection, training, and placing of workers in addition to developing working processes based upon the movement of man. Through that work,

Laban developed the effort graph as a means of recording the kinesthetic quality of individual performance in industry.

In 1946, the Laban Art of Movement Guild was formed. That guild supported the movement training center for movement study and educational dance based upon Laban's concepts. Laban lectured on a regular basis at his studio, and at the same time, he lectured at colleges and universities.

In 1953, Laban moved to Addlestone, Surrey, where he established archives for his own work and the work of the Art of Movement Studio. In 1954, the Laban Art of Movement Centre was formed as an educational trust to perpetuate his work and to promote and provide education in the art of movement. He continued to work at Addlestone until his death in 1958.

Philosophical Basis of the Work of Laban

For Laban, the act of moving was a link between the physical and mental experiences of life. He believed that through the act of moving, one experienced an interaction of mind and body. He also believed that movement was everywhere; movement could be seen, organized, and understood in a still leaf, in a child at play, in a simple walk, and through all aspects of our daily lives.

To Laban, the central issue underlying the understanding of movement was that persons needed to visually, physically, and internally experience the energy of movement and then develop the ability to describe those movement experiences. He believed that after helping a person recall experiences from his or her "movement thinking," that person could enrich his or her movement vocabulary by experiencing similar experiences. For example, Laban believed that a person could recall movement experiences from earlier in life. The person could (a) be helped to recall the total experience of skipping, (b) be guided to make a self-analysis of the skipping, and (c) provide a vocabulary that describes the experience of skipping to heighten the skipping experience. Laban believed that everyone experiences all the subtleties and complexities of movement during early childhood but that not everyone recalls all of those movements in later life.

Part of the Laban movement analysis is to identify which specific movement experiences a person is not recalling and then provide prescriptive movement instruction to reawaken those movements in that person. Those who instruct and guide movement must have a comprehensive variety of movement experiences themselves to effectively diagnose, prescribe, and teach movement. Moreover, to teach movement with meaning, movement experiences should be guided through the use of specific movement themes, known as the **Efforts in Combination.** While Laban never made an application of these principles to music, since 1979 it has been my work to extend his philosophy into the various aspects of music making.

The Laban Effort Elements: Flow, Weight, Time, and Space

Movement is more than a change of location of the body or a change in the position of the body limbs. There are changes in speed, changes in direction, changes in focus, and changes in the energy associated with different movements. Consequently, there is a constant fluctuation in levels of exertion. Laban defined exertion in movement as the *interrelationship of flow, weight, time,* and *space,* which he called the **Effort Elements.** For each of the four Effort Elements, Laban identified a pair of extremes, which he called "qualities," with the idea that the quality of each element of a given movement could be described in relation to its placement on a continuum that extends between those two extremes.

Flow is the variation in the quality of bodily tension that underlies all of the Effort Elements. The extremes of flow are free and bound. **Free flow** allows body energy to move through and out beyond the body boundaries without any restriction. Ideal free flow movement is difficult to stop. A person experiencing total free flow would be difficult to stop, weightless and unhampered by tension. **Bound flow** movement is restrained and can be stopped easily; it forces the mover to contain energy within the body boundary. A person experiencing extreme bound flow would be tense to the point of motionless. Between the two extremes of free flow and bound flow are infinite gradations of tension.

Weight is the sensation of force or burden exerted in a movement. The extremes of weight are light and heavy. **Light movement** can be described as delicate and overcomes the sensation of body weight. **Heavy movement** is forceful and uses the sensation of body weight to make an impact. A person must sense the quality of his or her movements as being either light or heavy. Central to one's understanding, and consequently to one's understanding of rhythm, is the ability to sense involuntary changes in one's own body weight as well as the ability to change weight at will.

Time relates to the expenditure or duration of time in a movement.

The extremes of time are sustained and quick. **Sustained time** is prolonging, lingering, or decelerating. **Quick time** contains a sense of urgency and rapidity. For musicians, the Effort Element of time is closely related to tempo.

Space is the manner in which energy is focused in a movement. The extremes of space are either direct or indirect. **Indirect movement** involves a flexible but all-encompassing attention to the environment. **Direct movement** involves a channeled, singularly focused awareness of the environment. The element of space is closely related to the concept of focus. Is the space in which a movement takes place focused or spread? Do all body parts focus to a central point, or are they dispersed?

One might think of the Effort Elements of flow, weight, time, and space as the how, what, when, and where of movement.

Experiencing the Efforts in Combination

It is easiest to gain an understanding of the Effort Elements through their various combinations as suggested by Laban. It is difficult to experience flow, weight, time, or space separately. By adjusting the relative intensities of flow, weight, time, and space within an activity, one can relate an infinite variety of movement possibilities. Laban assigned an action verb to each combination of three of the Effort Elements. Central to his theory is the simultaneous concentration on the three elements of weight, space, and time taking over, or predominating, changes in flow. Laban's action verbs, which describe combinations of the Effort Elements, along with movement examples for each verb are shown on the next page. The abbreviations denote S = Space, W = Weight, and T = Time.

For each of the Efforts in Combination, the elements of time, space, and weight interact to produce the illusion of flow. That is, the perception of one's rhythmic and gestural flow is a by-product of the interaction of time, space, and weight. Flow cannot exist alone. It is the result of infinite combinations of time, weight, and space, which produces an infinite variety of movement. The genius of Laban is the ability to observe how the combinations of time, space, and weight can be varied to produce what is perceived as flow. These principles are important to conductors to make them aware of the infinite potential of their own movement and to reawaken movement within themselves that may not have been used since childhood, or to reawaken movement that may not be part of their current life experience.

Laban Efforts in Combination to Describe Movement

Laban Action Verb (Elements)	Qualities	Movement Examples
float	indirect (S) light (W) sustained (T)	treading water at various depths
wring	indirect (S) heavy (W) sustained (T)	wringing a beach towel
glide	direct (S) light (W) sustained (T)	smoothing wrinkles in a cloth
		ice skating
press	direct (S) heavy (W) sustained (T)	pushing a car
flick	indirect (S) light (W) quick (T)	dusting off lint from clothing
slash	indirect (S) heavy (W) quick (T)	fencing
		serving a tennis ball
dab	direct (S) light (W) quick (T)	typing
		tapping on a window
punch	direct (S) heavy (W) quick (T)	boxing

Laban believed that to become adept with movement, one should develop a daily routine of exploring the Efforts in Combination. In the initial stages of movement exploration, the "labeling" and understanding of the Effort Element content in everyday life activities provide the foundation of movement understanding because it grows out of one's personal experience. Laban believed that we have all experienced a complete spectrum of movement possibilities as children, but we have forgotten those movement experiences because the routine of our daily lives has minimized our daily movement experience. For each of the Combinations shown on the previous page, there are suggestions of life activities that would reawaken that particular Effort Combination within the conductor. Mime each of the suggestions for each category and discover how a change in one or more of the individual Effort Elements changes the movement. Add your personal experiences to each list.

EXPERIENCES OF EFFORTS IN COMBINATION

Float
indirect (space)
light (weight)
sustained (time)

- tracing a picture with a pencil
- floating in a pool on your back
- vaulting over a high bar by means of a pole
- using a bubble wand
- spraying a room with air freshener
- lying on a waterbed
- falling into the first moments of sleep
- reaching for an unfamiliar cat
- staggering
- swinging on a rope swing
- blowing bubbles
- Other:

Wring
indirect (space)
heavy (weight)
sustained (time)

- twisting a washcloth dry
- twisting a sweater dry
- twisting hair in the morning
- twisting a face cloth
- drying out a sponge
- twisting off a bottle cap

- opening a cardboard can of prepackaged cookie dough
- washing socks
- playing with a hula hoop
- drying your hands under a blower
- tightening a jar cap
- turning over dirt with a trowel
- squeezing juice from an orange
- twisting a twist tie on a garbage bag
- using a screwdriver
- pulling out the stem of an apple
- spinning a dreidel
- opening a can of sardines
- using a melon baller
- opening a stuck faucet handle
- massaging a muscle
- Other:

Press
direct (space)
heavy (weight)
sustained (time)

- kissing a child gently
- pushing a shopping cart loaded with groceries
- ironing a shirt
- pressing a button on a drink machine
- pushing a child on a swing
- squeezing a tennis ball
- pressing on the floor when doing a handstand
- closing an overloaded suitcase
- pushing a lawnmower in high grass
- pushing a lawnmower up hill
- using a paper cutter
- using a hole punch
- pushing in a laundromat coin cartridge
- moving a piano
- pedaling a mountain bike up hill
- applying the brakes on a car
- kneading dough for bread

- removing a childproof cap
- walking with an umbrella against the wind
- washing a window with a squeegee
- stapling papers
- using a clothespin
- ringing a doorbell
- pushing in a thumbtack
- using a screwdriver
- packing trash in a filled garbage bag
- using a mechanical hand drill
- going through a revolving door
- closing a car trunk lid when the trunk is very full
- making mashed potatoes
- buckling a seat belt
- Other:

Glide
direct (space)
light (weight)
sustained (time)

- reaching to shake hands
- wiping up a spill with a paper towel
- pushing off from the side of a pool and moving forward
- ice skating
- erasing a blackboard
- dusting or wiping off a table
- drawing a violin bow across one string
- spreading butter or jelly on toast
- gently scratching your arm
- sliding down a banister
- coasting down a hill on a bicycle
- roller-blading or roller-skating
- throwing a paper airplane
- sliding in socks on a newly polished floor
- painting a wall with a roller
- opening a sliding glass door
- smoothing the sheets when making a bed
- dusting furniture with a feather duster

- putting a ring on your finger
- closing a zip-lock sandwich bag
- turning a page in a book
- smoothing cement with a trowel
- water skiing or snow skiing
- icing a cake
- drawing a circle with a compass
- playing a glissando on a piano
- sliding on an icy sidewalk
- shaving
- Other:

Dab
direct (space)
light (weight)
quick (time)

- putting the final touches on the frosting of a cake
- tip-toeing
- playing darts (moment the dart is released from the hand)
- using a paint brush to make dots
- poking someone's arm with a finger
- dipping a cloth in a pail of water
- breaking a balloon with a pin
- knocking ash off a cigarette
- dotting an "i"
- applying antiseptic on a small cut
- tap-dancing
- pushing a button on a remote control
- typing
- finger-painting
- using touch-up paint
- testing hot water with your finger
- cleaning cobwebs from the ceiling
- powdering on make-up
- using white glue
- cleaning a child's sticky mouth
- placing a cherry on a sundae
- Other:

Flick
indirect (space)
light (weight)
quick (time)
- removing an insect off the table
- turning a light switch on or off
- leafing through the pages of a book
- lightly keeping a balloon in the air
- brushing debris off a desk or table
- shooing a fly
- wiping sweat from the brow
- shooting marbles
- touching a hot stove
- throwing a frisbee
- snapping your fingers
- opening "flip-top" toothpaste
- brushing snow from a windshield
- lighting a cigarette lighter
- taking a basketball foul shot
- striking a match
- folding egg whites
- throwing rice
- popping soap bubbles
- Other:

Slash
indirect (space)
heavy (weight)
quick (time)
- swinging a baseball bat
- fencing
- casting a fishing line
- golfing
- opening a cardboard carton with a utility knife
- wielding a knife like a butcher
- tearing a piece of paper
- using an axe to chop wood
- slamming a door

- shaking catsup from a new bottle
- employing self-defense maneuvers
- sweeping a sandy floor with a push broom
- beating a hanging rug clean
- cutting vegetables
- Other:

Punch
direct (space)
heavy (weight)
quick (time)
- plumping a pillow
- boxing
- using a punching bag
- applauding loudly
- hammering a nail
- pounding a fist on a table
- striking a stapler to get the staple in a hard wall
- digging a hole
- Other:

Application of Laban Efforts in Combination to Musical Phrase and Direction of Musical Line

Notice that a variation of one or more of the qualities will result in a different intensity of the movement experience. After experiencing the Efforts in Combination shown above, the reader is encouraged to perform the imagery exercise below. Without pause, the reader should perform quickly each pair of movements shown. If the exercises are performed correctly, the mover will feel a sudden shift of energy between the two movement experiences of each pair. Each exercise should be performed first with external body movement and then with no external body movement so the mover can internalize the various combinations of movements and, more important, the changes in energy between the two movements in each combination. The quality of the time element of each of the movements should be varied, as should the direction of each movement.

Laban did not specifically assign names to each of the combinations listed below. The terms "flick," "dab," etc., have grown from the wide body of Laban practitioners who have found these labels useful and in keeping with the integrity of Laban's philosophical beliefs. Laban believed that language could be more exacting about the action than it could be for the more subtle shades of experience. Transitions occur when one moves between effort actions by changing one of the Effort Elements. For example, one may progress from punching (direct/heavy/quick) to pressing (direct/heavy/sustained). Transitions often involve the changing of a single component; it is possible, however, to change two or three components simultaneously.

Movement Imagery Exercise

    Punch/Press

    Punch/Slash

    Punch/Dab

    Slash/Wring

    Slash/Flick

    Wring/Float

    Wring/Press

    Float/Flick

    Float/Glide

    Glide/Dab

    Glide/Press

    Dab/Flick

When proceeding through the various **Core Vocal Exercises** later in this book, always listen for musical line—that is, whether the vocalic flow of the choir is moving forward. If not, there are several possible solutions for this problem. The use of one or all of them may be used.

One could consider associating movement with the sung vocalize. Many times, however, the lack of forward motion could be attributed to a lack of knowledge or fantasy concerning the shape of the phrase. To accomplish this, one may affix the appropriate Effort in Combination to the appropriate portion of the phrase. For example, in a four-bar musical example, one might tell the choir to feel "two bars of float and two bars of press." Depending on the musical intent of both the music and the conductor, appropriate Laban efforts can be associated with a musical phrase to bring about the desired movement within the phrase being sung.

Summary

In singing, Laban's theories of movement can help singers reacquaint themselves with their movement potential. Rhythm, which comes from a source within us, can be manifest as external movement. That external movement can be labeled to help us appreciate the infinite possibilities and experiences of rhythm manifest as movement. Rhythm is a manifestation of tension and release that provides points of reference commonly referred to as "meter." Rhythm phrases, then, are movement manifestations of the Efforts in Combination. But more importantly, a realization of the energy of the Effort Elements within oneself is actually a manifestation of color through rhythm.

The vocal color of a choir is directly affected by one major factor: the **breath** of the singers. Within that breath, the rhythmic life of the piece is transferred to the choir. The rhythmicity of the breath transfers rhythmic opinions and biases concerning phrase direction directly to the choir. That rhythmic (movement) vocabulary can be expanded through one's facility with the Efforts in Combination.

PART VII

BUILDING CONSISTENT TEMPO SKILLS THROUGH THE CHORAL WARM-UP

Chapter 17
Strategies for Teaching Rhythm

Building rhythm skills within a choral ensemble requires patient, diligent, and consistent pedagogical effort on the part of the conductor. Surely, a choir's rhythmic ability is directly related to the singers' inherent music aptitude as measured with a standardized aptitude test. However, regardless of the aptitude level, rhythm performance skill can be maximized through a logical and consistent approach to teaching the concept of consistent tempo. Consistent tempo is the grammar of rhythm. Without consistent tempo, the choir will be unable to process and organize the rhythm they hear and feel.

Most conductors have been taught to teach and correct rhythm problems by simply echoing or repeating the rhythm back after the conductor's example. This is imitation. Imitation is imitation. The choir will imitate the rhythm without any rhythmic or kinesthetic understanding. Likewise, clapping a rhythm is a futile effort because it is an exercise in imitation. Simple clapping and simple verbal repetition should never be used as devices for correcting or teaching any aspect of rhythm. Central to the learning and consequent understanding of rhythm as a performance tool is to be taught rhythm using the layered structure in which we hear and organize rhythm.

Choral warm-ups must be sung in consistent tempo. Consistent tempo is central to rhythmic, energized breathing. Rhythmic pulse is established and initiated with breath that, in and of itself, is rhythmic. Once breath is taken within the structure of a tempo, it is the responsibility of the singer to maintain that consistent tempo. I often refer to Robert Shaw's often-used admonition to many choirs: "I am out of the tempo business...that is **your** responsibility."

So how does one build such a skill within the choir? Through a consistent way of "inputting" the three distinct layers of rhythm—simultaneously! One should never allow warm-up exercises to be sung with fluctuating tempo. If fluctuating tempo is allowed in the warm-up, then it most certainly will creep into the performance literature. Once the problem is manifest in the performance literature, then it is more problematic to correct and wastes valuable rehearsal time. The teaching of consistent tempo is best accomplished during the warm-up period.

Rhythm teaching is hierarchical. That is, one must be coordinated before one can organize and feel the structure of rhythm. If a choir cannot maintain a consistent tempo, the ability to perform simple coordinated movements should be examined. Those coordinated muscle movements, once taught and drilled, will allow for a higher level of music learning to take place. Remember that ultimately, all rhythm is learned kinesthetically. Without the ability to organize the large beats of music through the feeling of body movement, the learning of rhythm becomes a mathematical exercise. Rhythm that is thought is never learned. Only rhythm that is felt and experienced will be retained and used.

Singing at a consistent tempo is a kinesthetic state and must be taught as such. Ensembles must learn to "feel" what it is like to sing in a consistent tempo. The choir must establish a "communal tempo" for rhythm to have an exciting life of its own. The ability to recognize and to perform a consistent tempo is a prerequisite to musical performance, and it is based upon one's ability to simultaneously hear a larger beat structure with its subdivision. An inability to recognize and perform a consistent tempo is rooted in one's inability to move in a coordinated manner to music. Before one learns about the larger beat structure with its subdivision, fine muscle coordination of the body must be achieved.

Muscle Coordination Development

Fine muscle coordination is developed separate from music listening abilities, which help aurally identify larger beats and their subdivisions. Muscle coordination is usually developed using an external music stimulus, such as a recording. After the necessary coordination has been developed, a music learning process that internalizes rhythm pulse becomes necessary. The following coordination sequence is based upon the work of Phyllis S. Weikart (1989). Coordination instruction moves through the following consecutive levels. Level 1 must be achieved before Level 2 can be attempted, and so on.

Movement Coordination Sequence

1.
Single Coordinated Motion of the Arms
↓
movement of both arms together

2.
Single Coordinated Motion of the Legs
↓
movement of both legs together

3.
Alternating Single Motion of the Arms
↓
movement of the arms alternately

4.
Alternating Single Motion of the Legs
↓
movement of the legs alternately

5.
Single Coordinated Motion of the Arms and Legs
↓
movement of both arms together and both legs together

6.
Alternating Single Motion of the Arms and Legs Together
↓
movement of the arms alternately and the legs alternately

When performing the coordination sequence above, observe the following:

1. Perform the various levels of the coordination sequence seated.

2. Until you have executed a level of the sequence accurately, do not supply an external beat.

3. After mastering a level as evidenced by a number of successful executions, perform that level with music. Perform each level at different tempi.

Rhythmic Response to External Music vs. Internal Musical Impulse

Many believe that if one can move to music, then one has demonstrated a certain rhythmic competency. Movement to music may be an indicator of a musical rhythmic understanding. It may also be an indicator that one is able to coordinate one's movements quickly to music that is heard with little or no musical understanding. Ultimately, until one demonstrates in solo without external music, one can never be sure of the origin or depth of one's rhythm responses. Traditional prescriptive rhythm exercises, such as clapping the beat or clapping the rhythm, may or may not indicate the extent to which someone hears rhythm.

How, then, can one be sure rhythm is "heard" internally? Many rhythm pedagogies make the error of **not** having a consistent "input" strategy to ensures that the singers "hear" all the component parts of the rhythm structure. The choir is bombarded with many teaching techniques that are well meaning but hopelessly confuse the choir and destroy their logic for the understanding of rhythm. The following approach attempts to create a consistent strategy.

The Structure of Rhythm and Its Relation to Rhythm Pedagogy

While most would agree on the importance of teaching and reinforcing rhythm skills, perhaps no aspect of music pedagogy has been subject to such confusion. Many attempts have been made to develop pedagogy for teaching rhythm, but that pedagogy lags behind the pedagogy for teaching tonal skills. Most music curricula limit rhythm content to relatively few patterns in duple and triple meters, and even then there is confusion about whether to teach those rhythm patterns using numbers for four sixteenth notes (e.g., "1–e–and–a") or using mnemonic devices (e.g., "Mississippi") for the same pattern. Whatever system is used, terminology is inconsistent, leaving a chasm of illogic for conductors between what is heard and what is written. While advanced musicians have suffered through and eventually reconciled those inconsistencies of rhythm notation, children and adults who have limited experiences with music are hopelessly confused by those same inconsistencies.

Natural Body Response to Rhythm: The Foundation for Understanding Rhythm

Between birth and age three, children learn without biases (and without notation). Their bodies move and respond to rhythm in a natural way. They play and experience rhythm and movement without inhibition. As adults, it is helpful to learn as a child learns music.

The core of rhythm learning must be based in movement. Consider the following controversial example. Audiate (hear the sound without it being physically present) *My Country 'Tis of Thee*. A music theorist might describe the tune as being in three-four time (three beats in a measure with a quarter note representing one beat). That is visually correct. However, there is a conflict between the measure signature and how the music is heard or audiated. Silently hear (audiate) *My Country 'Tis of Thee* again, but this time move to music. Do you move on each quarter note? Probably not. Do you step or move once each measure? Probably. Is it amusical to step to each quarter note? Yes. Would children step to each quarter note? They most likely would not.

The learning of rhythm must be organized and based upon the body's response to audiated rhythm, free of notation. Rhythm learning should be rooted not in the theory of music, but in its audiation. While the theory of music is important to the explanation of the common practice of a given period, it is not necessary for the learning of rhythm. In the same way the reading of individual letters and the principles of grammar are not necessary for speaking or reading a language, the knowledge of note values and the theory of meter signatures does not directly bear upon the beginning stages of rhythm learning. However, a body that responds naturally to rhythm is a necessary prerequisite for the learning of rhythm and the establishment of consistent tempo.

Layers of Rhythm Audiation

Rhythm, when audiated with understanding, is heard at three different levels concurrently. For the purpose of this explanation, consider the three levels as layers of audiation—that is, rhythm is audiated in relation to three separate elements. To audiate rhythm, one must organize rhythm patterns either consciously or unconsciously, but organization must take place at some level. For very talented students, the organization at more basic levels takes place unconsciously.

The three elements of rhythm are shown on the next page. The **macro beat,** the largest unit of pulse to which the body can move comfortably, is at the bottom of the chart, indicating that it is fundamental to rhythm audiation. **Micro beats** are the principal subdivisions of the macro beat; the macro beat is divisible into either two or three micro beats (except in the rare case of an intact macro beat). While the macro beat is fundamental to rhythm audiation, consistent tempo cannot be established without the concurrent audiation of macro and micro beats. Macro beats and micro beats must be audiated separately and then combined in audiation. They are not audiated separately before being combined, each loses its fundamental character and relationship to the other. The result is inconsistent tempo.

Melodic rhythm is the third layer of rhythm audiation. Melodic rhythm cannot be audiated with meaning and with consistency of tempo unless the previous two layers of rhythm are being audiated concurrent to it. Melodic rhythm is superimposed over the micro beat layer which, in turn, has been superimposed over the macro beat layer. Melodic rhythms can be categorized according to one or a combination of two or more of the following descriptive terms:

- Divisions
- Elongation
- Rests
- Ties
- Upbeats

Combinations of those functions constitute the rhythm of the melody, which is superimposed over the audiation of macro and micro beats. Rhythm audiation is, therefore, a threefold hearing process. Of the three layers of rhythm "hearing," the most crucial (if not the most fundamental), is the middle layer. Without the ability to accurately place micro beats, one will know only unusual meter and will never experience the feeling of consistent tempo.

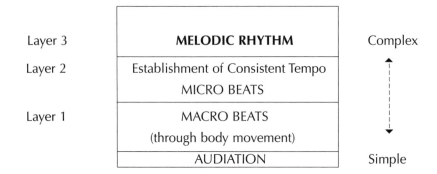

What is the practical application toward the development of rhythm skills in the choral ensemble? Consider the performance of the following rhythm pattern in a sequence of rhythm patterns: two eighths–two eighths–four sixteenths–two eighths. You perform the rhythm but rush the sixteenth notes. Now consider the suggested threefold layering of rhythm audiation above. How should you correct the rushed tempo?

1. Move your body to macro beats at a consistent tempo while chanting micro beats (eighth notes), emphasizing an equal subdivision of the beat. Continue that procedure until you sense a consistent tempo.

2. When a consistent tempo has been established, then add the third layer of rhythm, the melodic rhythm.

3. Remember that the strongest indicator of correct rhythm audiation is a person's sense of consistent tempo. If a consistent tempo is not present, remove each layer of rhythm audiation, beginning with melodic rhythm, until the problem is solved.

4. Then rebuild the layers back through melodic rhythm as long as consistency of tempo is maintained.

The strength of this approach to rhythm is that it separates the audiation of rhythm into three distinct layers and reveals that melodic rhythm is superimposed over two more fundamental rhythm elements which, together, provide a foundation for consistent tempo.

The Role of Consistent Tempo in Music Performance

One of the problems when initially learning a new work is the lack of persistence to maintain consistent tempo when learning individual parts or the work as a whole. Consequently, in subsequent study sessions of the work, the tempo is more subject to flux based on the lack of a rhythmic anchor—a consistent tempo that comes from within us.

In the initial stages of learning a piece, follow the guidelines below:

1. **Walk the room to step and rhythmically chant the piece or exercise to find the macro beat.** Walk about the room and step the rhythmic example while you chant it on a neutral syllable (such as "bum," "doo," "pah," etc.). The pulse you most naturally step to (regardless of the meter signature) is the macro beat, or the largest rhythm unit of the work. Remember that the unit of pulse you step to **may not** be the unit of pulse signified by the meter signature. Always rely on what you hear, not on what you see on the printed page. If you have any difficulty doing this, perform the movement coordination sequence discussed previously in this chapter under "Muscle Coordination Development."

2. **Locate the micro beat in your hands while concurrently tapping the macro beat in your feet.** After walking the exercise, be seated. Tap the beat you just stepped in your feet. While chanting the exercise, determine whether the beat in your feet can be divided into twos or threes by lightly tapping your index and middle fingers of your right hand on your upturned left palm. The division of the macro beat into the next smaller subdivisions is known as the micro beat.

3. **Chant through the exercise, breathing for each entrance.** Continue tapping the macro beat in your feet and the micro beat in your hands. Rhythmically chant the entire exercise on a neutral syllable, taking care to breathe for each entrance. Inconsistent tempo problems are most often caused by non-rhythmic breathing. Rhythmic breathing, key to a choir's consistent tempo, grows out of an inner consistent tempo of the conductor that is rooted in the concurrent macro and micro beats.

4. **Chant through the exercise without tapping.** Remove the tapping of the macro beats in the feet and the micro beats in the hands,

and rhythmically chant the piece while still breathing for each entrance. This will determine whether the consistent tempo of the piece is anchored within your audiation. If you have difficulty doing this, repeat Steps 1–3 until the tempo stabilizes.

Using a Metronome to Establish Communal Kinesthetic Tempo

A metronome is an invaluable tool for allowing the choir to experience the feeling of consistent tempo. Many of the problems associated with rushing and slowing have to do with the inability of the choir to be aware of the kinesthetic that is felt and perceived when singing at a consistent tempo. Many believe that the way to accomplish this is to teach music theory. However, teaching the reading of rhythm has very little effect on a person's ability to perceive, feel, and organize the rhythm that is heard. What one needs to teach and constantly reinforce is the feeling that accompanies the "state" of consistent tempo.

The process is relatively simple.

1. As the choir sings an exercise, simply turn on an aural metronome. I prefer to use the TAMA Rhythm Watch (A-100).

2. Have the metronome click both the macro beat and its first subdivision, the micro beat.

3. After the metronome is sounding, have the choir sing with the metronome. You will find that this allows the ensemble to experience the feeling of consistent tempo.

4. As soon as the ensemble begins to rush, stop them and ask them to listen again to the metronome.

5. Repeat this procedure until the tempo is consistent and stabile.

Remember that maintenance of consistent tempo is the responsibility of each individual choir member. Always correct consistent tempo problems in the same way each time they occur! The use of the metronome forces rhythmic responsibility upon the ensemble, plus it awakens the choir to the kinesthetic of consistent tempo. Once consistent tempo is established, and the three layers of rhythm are audiated, true rhythmic learning and understanding can take place. All of this can be accomplished during the choral warm-up.

PART VIII

CONSTRUCTING YOUR WARM-UP

Chapter 18
Rehearsal Planning Template

> When the director is thoroughly prepared, the rehearsal will be better, the work will require less time to learn, and the result will be an artistic and secure performance. Remember that the choir must suffer the consequences of each sin of omission on the part of the director! (p. 150)
>
> Wilhelm Ehmann
> *Choral Directing*

In the initial stages of learning to plan an efficient warm-up, it is important to use a standard template to "cut and paste" exercises so the pedagogical order of the exercises is always the same. After planning the warm-up using this guide, transfer the essential exercises to no more than two 5x7 cards.

1. Complete an analysis of the pieces you will use in the rehearsal that day to determine the mode (major, Dorian, Phrygian, etc.).

2. Design or select relaxation activities for the choir. These should be limited to no more than two minutes.

3. When aligning the choir, use Body Mapping vocabulary and imagery. It is important to pre-select the phrases you will use to remind the choir of the core of the body and the points of balance. Phrases to employ can be found on the alignment cards included at the back of this book.

4. Remember to sigh and then diagnose the healthiness of the "sighed" sound.

5. Choose appropriate inhalation and exhalation activities, and employ eight-handed breathing to reinforce the movement of air into and out of the body.

6. **Always** employ resonance-generating exercises using humming and chewing in all registers. Do this during every warm-up.

7. Before you begin vocalizing the choir, decide what type of resonance (tall and narrow vowels or round vowels) will be necessary for the literature to be rehearsed.

8. Next, choose appropriate exercises from the **Core Vocal Exercises** from this book that correspond to the vocal objectives you wish to teach (e.g., legato, marcato, leaps, etc.) and record the number of the exercise in the appropriate box on the template. Carry the "tune" of the chosen exercises into the rehearsal using the melodic cue cards at the back of this volume. Use the cards as a reminder of the appropriate teaching procedures for each vocal technique.

9. Select any specific exercises that are particular or unique to the piece you are rehearsing.

10. **Before beginning the music portion of rehearsal, be certain not to omit the aural transition exercises.** Exercises that are in the mode of the piece(s) to be rehearsed must be prepared aurally through the use of at least two exercises from *Ear Training Immersion Exercises for Choirs* (Jordan and Shenenberger, GIA Publications, 2004). You must do aural immersion exercises even if the piece you will be rehearsing is major. You must do at least two intonation exercises and are encouraged to perform one of the interval exercises.

11. Remember to always sigh between exercises!

To make certain you understand how to use the planning template presented on the following pages, a completed template for a rehearsal is included to lead you through the process (see page 213). Remember that exercises for the vocalise portion of the warm-up are chosen from the **Core Vocal Exercises** for this book. You may choose unison exercises from other sources or compose the exercise yourself. Remember, however, that if you do this, you may find it difficult to reinforce good pitch through a harmonic surrounding.

Important Note:
If you choose unison exercises, make sure your accompanist plays the dominant in alternating octaves above the tessitura of the choir.

Warm-Up Planning Template

Rehearsal Date:

Works to Be Rehearsed:

                Title   Mode

Relaxation Activity:

Establish Six Points of Balance:

DIAGNOSTIC SIGH ("oo" or "ee")

Body Mapping for Inhalation/Exhalation:

Body Mapping Reinforcement Phrases (from breathing cards)
to be used to support above activity:

Inhalation/Exhalation Activity:

SIGH

Resonance Exercise:

NOTE: The above must be done every warm-up.

GENERAL EXERCISES

Legato Exercise (selected from Core Vocal Exercises):

Legato with Leap (selected from Core Vocal Exercises)

SIGH

Range Extension (selected from Core Vocal Exercises)

GENERAL EXERCISES *(continued)*

Alignment and Breath Reinforcement Phrases for Use in Range Extension Exercises

Legato (selected from Core Vocal Exercises)

SIGH

SPECIFIC EXERCISES FOR WORKS IN REHEARSAL

Work:

Work:

Specific Exercise One

SPECIFIC EXERCISES *(continued)*

Specific Exercise Two

SIGH

CHORAL ENSEMBLE WARM-UP: SECTION TWO

Aural Immersion Exercises

Intonation Exercise (self-designed)

SIGH

Warm-Up Planning Template

Rehearsal Date:

Works to Be Rehearsed:

Title	Mode
Bruckner, Pange Lingua (GIA G-6481)	Phrygian

Relaxation Activity:

(1) Mirrored Mime: Ask the choir to imitate your movements as if they were looking in a mirror. Make sure to use all areas of body space in this activity.
(2) Reach for the ceiling; reach for the floor.
(3) Give yourself a tight hug, then relax. Repeat.
(4) Shake your arms like a horizontal windmill.

Establish Six Points of Balance:

(1) Ask the choir to point to the hips. Then ask them to locate the A/O joint and gently move the head as if they were saying "yes."
(2) Ask the choir to imagine length between points 4 and 1 (hips and A/O joint).
(3) Ask the choir to check with the position of their feet.
(4) Etc.

DIAGNOSTIC SIGH ("oo" or "ee")

Body Mapping for Inhalation/Exhalation:

Which part or parts of eight-handed breathing will be reviewed?

(1) Review the action of the diaphragm by asking the choir to hold their hands in the position of moving from "more domed" to "less domed."
(2) Review the action of the excursion of the ribs by having the choir use their hands as "excurting" ribs.

Body Mapping Reinforcement Phrases (from breathing cards)
to be used to support above activity:

(1) Remember that your breath moves in a wavelike motion from top to bottom.
(2) Remember to breathe through your "front" tube.

Inhalation/Exhalation Activity:

Gestures that support breath coming into body like a wave

(1) Use the hands, mirroring a balloon as one inhales.
(2) Place one hand by the navel to simulate the depth of the inhalation.

SIGH

Resonance Exercise:

_____	Tall, narrow vowel (cool breath)
x	Round vowel (warm breath)

Any supportive gestures?
Use hand on forehead.

_____	Humming and chewing in all registers with hand on forehead
_____	Upward and downward glissandi on "ng"
_____	Other

NOTE: The above must be done every warm-up.

Legato Exercise (selected from Core Vocal Exercises):

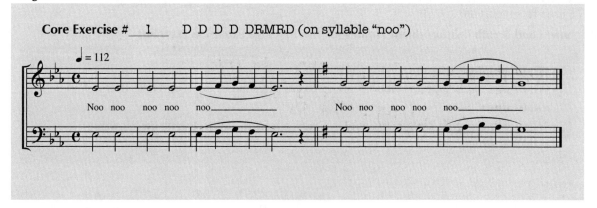

Legato with Leap (selected from Core Vocal Exercises)

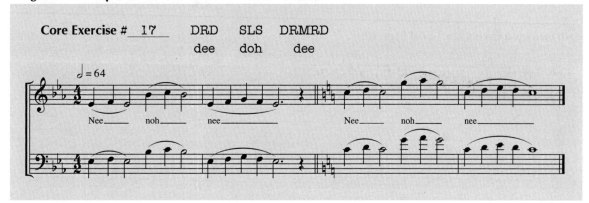

SIGH

Range Extension (selected from Core Vocal Exercises)

GENERAL EXERCISES *(continued)*

Alignment and Breath Reinforcement Phrases for Use in Range Extension Exercises

(1) When you are using air to sing, your spine lengthens, like a cat pouncing.
(2) When you breathe, your ribs do not expand; they make **outward** and **inward excursions**.
(3) When you take the breath for each phrase, breathe leaving your swallowing muscles alone.

Legato (selected from Core Vocal Exercises)

Core Exercise #_____

SIGH

SPECIFIC EXERCISES FOR WORKS IN REHEARSAL

Work: Bruckner: Pange Lingua

Work:

Specific Exercise One

Core Exercise #__4__ (Slow Tempo) 1 2 3 4 3 2 1

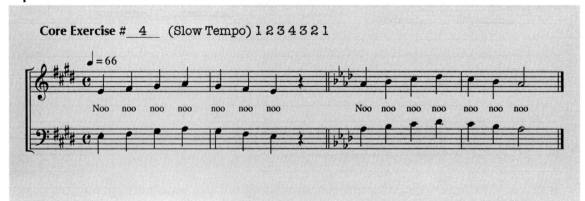

Noo noo noo noo noo noo noo   Noo noo noo noo noo noo noo

SPECIFIC EXERCISES *(continued)*

Specific Exercise Two

SIGH

CHORAL ENSEMBLE WARM-UP: SECTION TWO

Aural Immersion Exercises

Mode: Phrygian

Immersion Intonation Exercise (students refer to Singer's Edition)
    Exercise No. 49
Optional Immersion Intonation Exercise (students refer to Singer's Edition)
    Exercise No. 50
Immersion Tuning Exercise (students refer to Singer's Edition)
    Exercise No. 51
Optional Immersion Intonation Exercise (students refer to Singer's Edition)
    Exercise No. 52

Intonation Exercise (self-designed)

SIGH

PART IX

TROUBLESHOOTING CHORAL ENSEMBLE PROBLEMS AND SUGGESTED SOLUTIONS

Chapter 19
Troubleshooting Chart

Compiled on the pages that follow is a list of possible problems that may enter into the choral rehearsal. Solutions are identified that have been discussed throughout the text. The reader is encouraged to revisit those sections of the text that pertain to the problem they are attempting to resolve if there is a question concerning teaching procedure.

Problem	Symptom	Solution
tempo rushes	- Choir is not breathing in a consistent tempo. - Choir does not sense consistent tempo with both macro and micro beats.	- Use the metronome to arrive at communal tempo. - Teach the feeling of consistent tempo using metronome. - Ask choir to listen "harder."
tempo slows	- Consonants are too long and carry too much vocal weight into sound.	- Use physical gesture to remedy: use tossing gestures to lighten sound. - Ask choir to sing with more energy. - Ask choir to sing with entire body.
choir singing off the breath	- Sound is harsh, edgy, strident. - Pitch is sharp. - Sound is loud, glasslike.	- Use physical gesture to reacquaint choir with a supported singing sensation. - Use Breath "Kneading" Exercise.
unable to diagnose vocal problem	- Severe pitch problem. - Unable to hear pitch core. - Sound is cloudy, overly dark, pressed.	- Try to imitate the sound with your own singing voice. The solution should be apparent. - Always check for spaciousness.
lack of musical line	- Airflow for singing may be impeded. - Lack of commitment and energy on the part of the singers. - Sound is dull. - Tempo is slow.	- Make certain the choir understands the shape and direction of phrases. - Apply physical gesture to music.

Problem	Symptom	Solution
initial attack tight, restricted, and not free	<ul><li>Breath and onset of tone is being interrupted by vocal mechanism tension.</li><li>Choir is uncertain about the tempo in which they are to sing.</li></ul>	<ul><li>Choir needs to breathe the shape of the first vowel.</li><li>Choir should breathe in tempo and style they should sing.</li><li>Have choir sigh and maintain space.</li><li>Add physical gesture to reinforce space.</li></ul>
poor intonation throughout all parts	<ul><li>Color of vowel cannot maintain pitch.</li><li>Lack of rhythmic pulse within the ensemble.</li><li>Vowels need to be closed.</li><li>Head tone vowels "oo" and "ee" are not pure.</li><li>Change between vowel sounds is too slow.</li><li>Vocal sounds are not spacious, high, and forward.</li></ul>	<ul><li>Bring all vowels high and forward.</li><li>Use physical gesture to assist.</li><li>Make certain "oo" and "ee" vowels are pure.</li><li>Rehearse piece on vowels only; make sure vowel changes occur quickly.</li><li>Check for the "cave."</li><li>Use metronome to reinforce consistent tempo and inner pulse.</li></ul>
no *piano* dynamic	<ul><li>Choir loses space on *piano* sounds.</li><li>Choir loses energy and commitment.</li><li>Vowel is too open.</li><li>Lack of total body awareness.</li></ul>	<ul><li>Maintain spaciousness on *piano* sound.</li><li>Close vowels.</li><li>Use vocabulary that will bring body awareness to rehearsal.</li><li>Ask choir to "give" more energy.</li></ul>

Problem	Symptom	Solution
pitch changes as choir sustains sound	<ul><li>Tongue position changes as vowel is being sustained.</li><li>Attack of pitch was out of tune.</li></ul>	<ul><li>Maintain same tongue position through sustained pitches.</li><li>Ask choir to hear pitch before they sing.</li><li>Ask choir to listen "harder," especially at ends of longer pitches.</li></ul>
vibrato enters a sectional sound	<ul><li>Pitch is questionable.</li></ul>	<ul><li>Ask all members of section to listen "harder."</li><li>Ask choir to listen to everyone except themselves.</li><li>Check for excessive tongue and jaw tension.</li></ul>
"ah" vowel is out of tune	<ul><li>Vocal sounds are spread and airy.</li></ul>	<ul><li>Vowel must be high and forward.</li><li>Use physical gesture to bring sound high and forward.</li></ul>
"eh" vowel is out of tune or lacks color	<ul><li>Vowel is too open.</li><li>Tongue is not in proper position for "eh."</li></ul>	<ul><li>Bring vowel more high and forward.</li><li>Close vowel.</li><li>Make certain tongue is in "eh" position.</li><li>Ask choir to sing "eh" in "house of ee."</li></ul>

Problem	Symptom	Solution
"ih" vowel is out of tune	■ Vowel is too open. ■ Tongue is not in proper position for "ih."	■ Bring vowel more high and forward. ■ Wrap lips around sound. ■ Close vowel. ■ Make certain tongue is in "ih" position.
"oo" vowel is not clear	■ Pitch problems evident. ■ Vowel sounds more like "uh." ■ Singers' lips do not look like "oo."	■ Ask choir to imagine a "pit" in their tongue. ■ Ask the choir to wrap their lips around the sound. ■ Hold index finger 6 inches from nose to bring vowel forward. ■ Use physical gesture to avoid "jowl vowel."
upward leaps out of tune	■ Edgy, pressed sound on top pitch. ■ Sound is not free. ■ Sound is open, airy.	■ Make vertical space on ascent of leap and wrap lips around the sound. ■ Use Breath "Kneading" Exercise. ■ Wrap lips around sound on top pitch. ■ Increase speed of air before upward leap.
downward leaps out of tune	■ Increase of dynamic on lower note. ■ Vowel in leap sounds swallowed, back.	■ Maintain sound that is high and forward, regardless of vowel sound. ■ Do not increase volume on descending leaps. ■ Use physical gesture to encourage high, forward singing.
choir sings out of tune when singing diphthongs	■ Sound is unfocused.	■ Have the choir sing only the first vowel. (The second vowel will be slipped in as the choir moves to the next syllable or word.) ■ Rehearse piece staccato.

Problem	Symptom	Solution
choral sound is too "fat"	■ Musical line seems labored.	■ Ask the choir to sing tall and narrow vowels or to sing "cool" vowels. ■ Ask choir to breathe a cool breath.
choral sound is too bright	■ Edgy, glasslike quality in sound. ■ Sound is "off the breath."	■ Ask the choir to sing round vowels or to sing "warm" vowels. ■ Make certain larynx is in a down and lower position. ■ Wrap lips around vowel. ■ Use Breath "Kneading" Exercise to cause choir to sing "on the breath."
soprano sound is extremely tight and pinched in upper register	■ Sound is overly bright and strident.	■ Have sopranos think "uh" into the sound to create more space in the sound. ■ In extreme tessitura, eliminate all consonants. ■ Use Breath "Kneading" Exercise to ensure "on the breath" singing.
men's sound is out of tune, pressed, and strident in the upper register	■ Men's sound seems loud, edgy.	■ Have male singers make more space for the sound, and ask them to wrap their lips around the sound. ■ Use Breath "Kneading" Exercise to ensure "on the breath" singing. ■ Make certain larynx is down and relaxed.

Problem	Symptom	Solution
overall choral sound is tight and restricted	▪ Pitch problems can be heard.	▪ Use the sigh to return the larynx to a relaxed position for singing. ▪ Release jaw and tongue tension. ▪ Use heightened/exaggerated speaking to reacquaint choir with spacious singing.
choir is unable to perform a crescendo, decrescendo, or both	▪ Not enough head tone in women's and treble voices. ▪ Choir is not making more space on the crescendo and is losing space on the decrescendo rather than simply closing the vowel.	▪ Make certain sounds are high and forward. ▪ Sing all vowel sounds in "house of oo." ▪ Close the vowel by rounding the lips.
choir pitch fluctuates	▪ Vibrato in sound.	▪ Have the dominant played above the choir in alternating octaves as they rehearse the literature or sing a vocalise. ▪ Re-examine seating arrangement of the choir. ▪ Use choral seating arrangement with alti in front row. ▪ Ask choir to listen to everyone else except themselves.
vowel colors inconsistent; pitch fluctuates	▪ No distinct difference between vowel sounds.	▪ Rehearse music staccato with text that is being used.

Problem	Symptom	Solution
diction lacks color and vibrancy	- Vowels are most likely too open and are not high and forward. - Pitch problems occur.	- Close vowels. - Ask choir to supply more energy into the sound. - Ask choir to sing with the whole body.
	- Choral sound "fuzzy," cotton-like.	- Make certain the choir is singing on the breath. - Make certain the choir is correctly mapped for inhalation and exhalation sequence.
"ee" vowel not clear	- Not enough head tone in sound. - Tongue not in "ee" position. - Tongue not gently anchored against lower teeth. - Vowel not sufficiently closed.	- Close vowel. - Make certain tongue is in "ee" position, with tongue anchored against lower jaw and teeth.
"oo" vowel veiled, cloudy	- "Oo" vowel begins to sound like "uh."	- Bring vowel high and forward. - Wrap lips around sound. - Imagine pit in center of tongue. - Use physical gesture to bring sound high and forward.
tempo slows in fast passages	- Vowel changes too slow. - Consonants too thick. - Lack of consistent tempo.	- Sing passage with pointing. - Rehearse with metronome.

Problem	Symptom	Solution
vowel sound very indistinct	■ Consonants prior to the vowel are improperly executed.	■ Sing on vowels only. ■ Make certain of tongue participation in all vowel sounds.
alto and bass/baritone sections consistently under pitch	■ Sound is cloudy and lacks energy.	■ Sound needs to be high and forward. ■ Use physical gesture to bring sound high and forward. ■ Ask singers to sing all vowels in "house of ee."
choir has difficulty singing an exercise in tune	■ Sound seems to lack focus.	■ Ask the choir to listen to everything else except themselves. ■ Sound the dominant in alternating ostinato over the top of the choir's sound. ■ Make certain the choir is "aurally" prepared if the music sung is modal. ■ Use Aural Immersion Exercises in warm-up. ■ Have accompanist sound dominant above the choir.
alto consistently move into chest voice	■ Palette does not stay raised.	■ Ask the choir to "sing in the same apartment" as their upper register. ■ Ask the choir to think space of a sigh.
"oo" and "ee" vowels are not clear	■ Pitch problems begin to occur.	■ Make sure tongue position is changing quickly enough between vowel changes. ■ Wrap lips around the sound.
passages with runs slowing and indistinct	■ Pitches cannot be heard in runs.	■ Review martellato singing techniques. ■ Re-sing every vowel in running passages.
musical ideas lack interest and imagination	■ Sound is dull, boring.	■ Use Laban terminology to clarify kinesthetic feeling of the phrase. ■ Make certain weak beats of bar are energized.

Problem	Symptom	Solution

sound of ensemble lacks energy and vitality	- Pitch problems begin to occur.
	- Consonants are not crisp.
	- Sound is labored, dull.
		- Revising Body Mapping and total awareness issues:
		
		   Are you aware of your whole body when singing?
		
		   Are you aware of your back?
		
		   Are you aware of the space that surrounds your body?
		
		   Sing with your whole body.
		
		   Are you aware of every square inch of skin on your body when you sing?
		
		   Can you give more energy?
		
		   Can you stay aware for the whole rehearsal?
		
		   Imagine a situation or experience in your life when you have been in an aware state.

syllables of words carry unnecessary accent	- Text does not sound natural. - No flexibility, fluidity in musical line.	- Make certain choir knows the location of each schwa in the text. - Make certain choir is muting those syllables by wrapping their lips around the sound.
schwas or unaccented, unstressed syllables are carrying excessive accent and are sung as open vowels	- Sound of choir affected. - Text cannot be understood.	- Identify the syllable in the word that is a schwa. - It is helpful to ask the choir to circle the schwa syllable in red. - Ask the choir to wrap their lips around the sound for the syllable that has been identified as the schwa. - Make certain the lips participate in the muting of the schwa. - Be certain the schwa sound does not become dark in color. Schwa sounds must be spacious, high, and forward.

Problem	Symptom	Solution
choral sound is not vibrant and healthy entering into rehearsal after warm-up	▪ Pitch problems occur in warm-up. ▪ Sound is cloudy and dull.	▪ Re-examine warm-up procedure for mixed steps in pedagogical sequence. Relaxation Alignment and Body Awareness Relaxation of the Vocal Tract: Relaxing the Jaw, Tongue, and Lips Creating Spaciousness (Use of the Sigh) Breathing Exhalation and Inhalation Support Resonance General Resonance Specific Resonance Vowel Development Hierarchy Register Consistency
choral sound is out of tune and generally not vibrant, especially on *forte* sounds	▪ *Forte* sounds are "loud" rather than full and resonant.	▪ Revisit points of balance **Six Points of Skeletal Balance** **Correct Map of the Hips** (The balance of the upper half of our body over the legs) **Correct Map of the A/O Joint** (The balance of our head on our spine at the center) **Correct Map of the Pelvis: The Core of the Body** (The balance of our thorax on our massive lumbar vertebrae at the center). **Correct Map of Shoulders** (The balance of our arm structures over our spines at the center) **Correct Map of the Knees** (The balance of our knees at the center) **Correct Map of the Feet** (The balance of our bodies on the arches of our feet at the center)

Problem	Symptom	Solution
choir is unable to maintain space when singing, especially in *piano* sounds	- Pitch difficulties. - Vowel sounds are dull.	- Revisit how to create space via the "cave." Finding the "Cave" 1. Have the choir feel for the fleshy cartilage at the front of their ear hole. Have them place a finger just forward of that point. 2. Once they have located that point, have the choir slowly drop their jaw until they feel an indentation or a "cave." 3. Ask the choir to create a small cave rather than a large one. A larger cave indicates a hyperextension of the jaw.
choir is unable to sustain phrases because of inadequate breath	- Pitch and color of choir is compromised.	- Review Body Mapping principles of inhalation and exhalation: Are you aware of your breathing? Breathing moves from the top down, not like a glass filling up. Remember that breathing moves into the body in a wavelike motion, from top to bottom. Breathe through your front tube (trachea), not the back tube (esophagus). Breathe without using your swallowing muscles. When you breathe, your ribs do not expand; they make outward and inward excursions. You breathe at breathing joints, and those breathing joints are in the back. When you take air in, your spine gathers, like a cat preparing to pounce. When you are using air to sing, your spine lengthens, like a cat pouncing. Remember what space your lungs occupy in your chest cavity. Your diaphragm works on inhalation. Leave the area alone to dome back up on exhalation. Experience the whole cylinder of your abdominal wall. Outward and downward release allow your spine to lengthen. As you sustain the phrase, is your spine **lengthening**?

Problem	Symptom	Solution
after warm-up, choral sound not resonant and vital	■ Sound is dull, unenergetic. ■ Sound of choir sounds "small" and pressed. ■ Vowel sounds are not vibrant or distinct.	■ Did you do enough resonance exercises in your warm-up? 1. Begin the exercise by asking the choir to "hum and chew" in their middle register on the consonants "MMMM." 2. Make certain the choir hums and chews with teeth apart and lips lightly together. 3. Make certain the hum and chew is spacious. Ask singers to check their "caves" (see "Teaching Procedure for the Sigh"). 4. Make certain the humming and chewing is high and forward. To ensure this is being done and the sound does not rest in the jowels, ask the choir to place the heel of their hand on their forehead as they hum and chew. 5. To make certain resonances are generated in all registers of the voice, ask the singers to hum and chew also in their upper register and their lower register. 6. To ensure there is enough head tone in the sound, it is often helpful to immediately follow each humming and chewing exercise with a downward sigh on "oo" and the appropriate supporting hand gesture (see "Spaciousness and Proper Vocal Production through the Use of the Sigh: Relaxation of the Vocal Tracts—Creating Space"). ■ To ensure there is enough head tone in the sound, it is often helpful to immediately follow each humming and chewing exercise with a downward sigh on "oo," with the appropriate supporting hand gesture (see Chapter 8).

Problem	Symptom	Solution
breaks in legato line	▪ Vocalic flow is not consistent and ongoing.	1. Use **"breath-kneading gesture"** to continually reinforce the connection forward moving breath to vocalic flow. 2. Have the choir **"moan"** the line. Continually remind the choir to be in a CONSTANT state of **AWARENESS**. They must be aware of their entire body as they sing. 3. Make certain that the choir understand where each musical phrase moves toward; i.e. text stresses, etc. 4. Use physical movement whenever possible to reinforce the kinesthetic of the line. Make the musical line a physical experience!
	▪ In situations where the vowel is repeated on repeated pitches or in running passages, ask the singers to "re-sing" the vowel on every pitch.	
diction problems producing frequent pitch problems	▪ Choir is consistently out of tune.	**Review and correct vowel colors in correct correction order** ▪ **OO and EE** ▪ Elimination of Diphthongs ▪ **AH** **EH and IH** ▪ Execution of Consonants Appropriate to Style
		▪ Rehearse staccato with text or with vowels only. ▪ Make sure voiced consonants are voiced with pitch. ▪ Check mode of piece. ▪ Use Aural Immersion Exercises to prepare modality of the music.

PART X

THE CORE VOCAL EXERCISES: HARMONIZED MELODIC FORMULAE FOR WARM-UPS

Note: The Core Vocal Exercises contained in this part of the book are also available in a separate accompanist edition (GIA #G-6397A). Additionally, the melodies for all of the Core Vocal Exercises are reproduced on reference cards, available separately from the publisher (GIA #G-6397I), for easy access and use in the warm-up.

Chapter 20
The Core Vocal Exercises

Introduction James Jordan

The exercises that follow form a core body of exercises that can be used to teach the various aspects of vocal technique presented in this book. I have found that teachers have asked for a collection of exercises that they can use as the central part of their warm-up.

Persons who are familiar with my work will notice a major departure in this volume from my previous publications with respect to the construction of these exercises. In the past, I was a strong advocate of unison, unaccompanied exercises. I have since come to appreciate and understand the pedagogical strength and effectiveness of accompanied exercises that are harmonically well constructed.

The reasons for this are several. First, by having harmonically rich exercises, you are providing an enriched aural diet for the choir. They will be aurally enriched by hearing these exercises in each rehearsal. Second, exercises that are harmonically and rhythmically well-constructed support the musical line and overall vocal technique of the choir. Accompaniments that are well constructed provide a rhythmic energy and harmonic support that builds healthy, engaged and supported singing.

I have suggested the specific pedagogical uses of these exercises. For exercises in the categories of martellato and range extension, those exercises are specific as to their use. In other exercises, however, the conductor should feel free to use the exercises for the pedagogical reasons that he/she determines for that rehearsal. It is important, however, to teach only one or two concepts with each exercise. If too many concepts are attempted to be taught within a particular exercise, the choir becomes confused as to its vocal purpose AND it is difficult to provide specific vocal corrections so that the sound of the choir can improve.

In the near future, a CD will be recorded that will have both correct vocal performances juxtaposed with incorrect examples. The purpose of this CD will be to provide an aural tutorial for conductors so that they can learn to listen in a diagnostic way, to facilitate giving correction and feedback to the choir.

Above all, make certain that the exercises are always sung musically, and that the choir listens at all times to the accompaniments.

Instructions for Conductor

1. **The Conductor needs to sing the exercise first for the choir without accompaniment.** The conductor should introduce the exercise to the choir first by singing it to the choir without accompaniment after the accompanist sounds a pitch for the exercise. The accompanist can then choose whether to play the introduction or to move directly into the exercise beginning after the double bar.

2. **Inform the accompanist before the start of the rehearsal what exercises have been selected and in what order.** Give the accompanist a note detailing which exercises are to be sung during that warm-up.

3. **Place identifying tabs on the exercises.** In order to locate the exercises quickly in a rehearsal, the accompanist should place numeric tags on the appropriate pages 1, 2, 3, etc., so that exercises can be quickly located in rehearsal.

4. **Be ready to provide vocal correction and help to the singers.** Immediate feedback is central to any sound vocal pedagogy. Use the teaching technique cards (available separately) to maintain both consistent and effective pedagogy. Constant reinforcement of vocal technique is necessary for healthy vocal technique to become habitual.

5. **Add physical gesture to ensure that singers are assuming responsibility for their singing.** The value of physical gesture to reinforce valuable vocal concepts cannot be overemphasized. Apply physical gestures as discussed in the text as prescriptive aids to remedy vocal problems.

6. **ALWAYS make certain that the choir breathes using the macro beat or large beat.** It cannot be emphasized enough how important a rhythmic and energized breath is to vibrant choral tone. If the choir encounters breathing problems, reinforce inhalation, exhalation and support principles. Eight-handed breathing as presented on the Evoking Sound video and as presented in the accompanying text is central to this process.

7. **Use Body Mapping terminologies to reinforce body awarenesses.** The conductor must constantly employ verbal reminders or cues for the singers to maintain alignment awareness. Alignment awareness is foundational to healthy, vibrant singing.

Introduction Marilyn Shenenberger

In serving as accompanist for the Westminster Chapel Choir, I endeavored to provide accompaniments for the warm-ups that supplied a rich harmonic canvas, while supporting the pedagogical objectives of the exercises. It is imperative that these exercises be played with nuance, line, and rhythmic integrity. Well-harmonized exercises enrich the aural vocabularies of each singer; properly voiced accompaniments encourage supported, seated singing; and rhythmically secure accompaniments have the ability to provide a healthy rhythmic impetus that can assist with the singing of forward-moving and energized musical line. In addition, the accompaniment can support the intonation of the choir, by incorporating the dominant ostinato principles that are advocated in both publications, *Choral Ensemble Intonation* (GIA, 2001) and *Ear Training Immersion Exercises for Choirs* (GIA, 2004). Exercises that are voiced with psychological forethought concerning how to guide the choir to listen can provide efficient musical instruction.

By writing out these exercises, we are hoping to take the mystery out of choral warm-ups, so that a quality warm-up can be a consistent beginning for every rehearsal. By having the notated accompaniments, the accompanist is free to listen more and think less about the theory behind the keyboard improvisation. When a substitute accompanist was needed for Dr. Jordan's Chapel Choir, we would ask one of the students to play the rehearsal. Their biggest apprehension was that of improvising the accompaniment, while modulating upward by half steps; and not in their wildest dreams had they ever contemplated modulating downward by half steps! The modulations are, therefore, written out for the accompanist, and should be practiced by all your accompanists, so they sound effortless in the choral rehearsal. All modulations are through the dominant of the new key, or by way of a diminished seventh chord. A consistent accompaniment is of great assistance to the conductor, and is necessary in providing stability for the beginning of each rehearsal.

The accompanist is a collaborative artist with the conductor, and in many ways, an equal partner in the pedagogical process of teaching a choir. Your singers will emulate the musicianship of their director. An accompanist who plays with nuance, musical understanding, a listening ear, and sensitiviy to the director's interpretation is the best resource a conductor can have to insure a high standard of musicality within the choir. While the accompanist is wordless in the rehearsal, a skilled accompanist can affect the musical line, expressivity, and musical awareness, in addition to intonation and rhythmic acuity, simply through the music they provide.

If the accompanist has an understanding of HOW the choir learns and how they hear, that person can provide constant and ongoing non-verbal musical instruction to the choir. Of course, this can only be successful if the choir is encouraged to listen constantly to the keyboard, and if the accompanist listens for what support the choir needs. Sometimes LESS is MORE. By this, I mean that the accompanist should provide only what's necessary for the choir to be successful. With a new exercise or new piece of music, it is often necessary to play what the choir is to sing, but we accompanists often make the mistake of playing that long after the choir can and should be singing it on their own. In the warm-up exercises, the choir sings the same two- or four-measure phrase seven or more times. When the exercise is brand new, it should be presented vocally by the director. It may then be necessary for the accompanist to play the choir's melodic line in the right hand through two or three keys at most, and should then play only the written accompaniment unless the choir is faltering with the melody.

The voicing of the specific accompaniments was done with the pedagogical objective in mind. Range extension exercises must provide a strong bass which simulates the support needed for singing in the upper register. Sostenuto or line exercises with repeated tones (which will tend to go flat) need to incorporate the fifth played an octave above what the choir sings, which will give them the aural anchor they need to sing in tune. Slow exercises should include subdivision in the accompaniment, so that the singers feel the pulsing necessary to keep the line moving forward. Repetitive interval exercises require a directional line in the accompaniment which infuses the exercise with tension toward the resolution. Exercises which incorporate rests need an accompaniment which instills a sense of direction, so the rests are active rests, not inactive, which will cause "off-the-breath" singing. The needs of the singer are the same, whether the choir is small or large, although the volume and intensity of the accompaniment will vary in proportion to the size of the choir. Boy choirs and all girl choruses will need a softer touch on the marcato and martellato exercises, as well as the Aeolian range extension exercise.

The CD that accompanies this volume incorporates my musical decisions on the playing of these exercises in addition to tempi that elect the best singing from the choir. Each exercise is recorded twice, once with a flute and cello playing the vocal line over the accompaniment, and once with the accompaniment only. The first track is included to demonstrate the music inherent in the exercise itself. (Singers often think the text is the sole determiner of the interpretation.) It is not recorded with voice, because we didn't want the singers to perceive that the "correct" way to sing it would be limited to a particular vocal timbre. The instrumentalists used in this recording are phenomenal musicians. Dawn Williams is the flautist with the Bel Canto Players of South Jersey. Robert Cafaro is a cellist with the Philadelphia Orchestra. This track may be used by directors of choirs with or without accompanists, as a musical teaching tool for both the accompanist and the choir. The second track, with only the piano accompaniment, may be used as the surrogate accompanist for choirs who don't have an accompanist other than the director. This will allow the director the capability to affect the sound through gesture, rather than as a floating head behind the keyboard, as well as providing the freedom for the director to concentrate on the sound of the choir, and accomplish the purpose of the warm-up. It should also be used as a reference by the accompanists in learning how to support the choir from the keyboard on these specific exercises.

Basic Rules for Accompanists

1. **Be musical!** Not all notes are created equal! The traditional piano student begins by learning the notes, finding the notes with facility, following the printed dynamics, and working the selection up to tempo. The instructor is usually the advisor to the nuances hidden within the blueprint of the printed page, but necessary to make the performance of the piece a musical experience for the performer as well as the listener. We are asking the accompanist to go beyond the traditional "piano player" role, and to become a pianist. They need to know how to bring out the music without the presence of their piano teacher, as we often ask them to demonstrate it for the whole choir! If your accompanists are piano players, rather than pianists, you will need to work with them outside of the rehearsal to help them read more than the notes, in order to make the music come alive.

2. **Listen at all times.** The accompanist should strive to listen at all times to the choir. By constantly listening, the accompanist will hear when singers are hesitant, unsure of the pitch, or have misheard the pitch, all of which indicate the need for their part to be reinforced.

3. **Play the exercises in a consistent tempo.** These exercises should be performed in the same tempo from the beginning to the end, with a slight ritardando possible nearing the final resolution. While it IS the choir's responsibility to maintain tempo, the accompanist can certainly influence the maintenance of tempo by keeping a rock solid beat, without playing metronomically. ANY DISRUPTION OF TEMPO UPSETS THE BREATHING PROCESS IN THE SINGERS. Once the breathing process is upset, a process that is controlled by exact and consistent tempo, other vocal problems will appear. Among the resultant problems, "off-the-breath" singing and high larynx are the most serious. Many of the accompaniments include subdivisions of the macro beat the choir is singing for this very reason.

4. **Physically breathe with the conductor on the preparatory beat.** This beat provides far more than tempo. It informs the accompanist and singers of the affect of the piece: the tone color and the dynamics.

5. **Think about the color of the exercises.** The touch of the pianist determines whether the sound will be warm, crisp, brittle, expansive, tentative, harsh, etc. This directly affects the choir's perception of the piece, and the color they will sing. One well-played section of a piece can convey more information than a ten-minute explanation. Directors should rehearse with the accompanists before the rehearsal to be sure the information conveyed is what is desired, and be vigilant that the quality of tone played continually reflects the tone quality desired in the ensemble!

6. **Observe pedaling as indicated.** Close observance of pedaling is important so that harmonies are clear, and that exercises have a rhythmic and acoustic clarity.

7. **Know what to supply in the accompaniment when the choir BEGINS to sing out of tune.** If the intonation begins to slip, the accompanist should play the fifth an octave above the choir. This may be done by oscillating between the fifth and the root, using the fifth and root in an Alberti bass pattern above the choir, or simply adding the fifth in octaves on beats 2 and 4. The piece will determine which pattern fits best, as well as determining whether the root is the resting tone of the passage, or the dominant. In the case of chromatic passages, it may be necessary to change the anchor tones often.

8. **Encourage vocal independence.** Voice parts will need to be played initially, but should be left out as soon as the singers are confident. At this time, the accompanist should play aural anchors while listening for parts that need occasional assistance. If the accompaniment provides harmonic information apart from doubling the voice parts, it may be helpful for the choir to hear it. If, however, it is discordant, allow the choir to become more familiar with their parts before adding the accompaniment.

9. **Surround your singers with quality sound.** The timbre and intonation of the piano will directly influence the sound of the choir. Consequently, it behooves any choir to have the finest piano in their rehearsal room and a piano that is in tune! The accompanist should check the piano and, if necessary, avoid playing notes that are seriously out of tune. This may mean playing one hand in a different octave for a week until the piano can be tuned. Be vigilant that the quality of tone being played directly reflects the tone quality desired in the ensemble!

Finally, and perhaps most importantly, the exercises should be played in such a way that evokes good singing, and is pleasurable for the singers no matter how often they are sung. And, above all, they must insure that all sounds made during the rehearsal, no matter how simple the melodic idea, are at all times musical and expressive.

CHORAL WARM-UP EXERCISES
Quick Overview

Each exercise is shown in beginning key and suggested ending key.
It is preferable for the instructor to sing the exercise in tempo for the choir before they sing it.
If the CD accompaniment is being used, the recorded introduction is the vocal line of the exercise.

> The thumbnail sketches are provided for use by the conductor to sing the initial introduction to the choir, as well as quick reference in planning the warm-up.

1. Legato; Line

2. Repeated tone with crescendo and decrescendo

3. Maintain SHF (Spacious, High, and Forward) in Low register

4. Legato at a Slow tempo

CHORAL WARM-UP EXERCISES – Quick Overview

5. Singing on breath through moving eighth notes

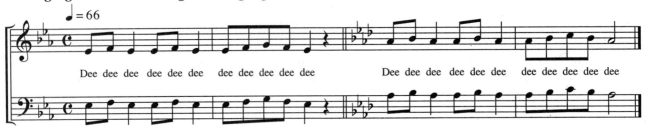

6. Register consistency with downward leaps

7. Range extension downward (Descends chromatically)

8. Range extension downward (Descends Chromatically)

9. Range extension upward and maintaining on-the-breath singing

CHORAL WARM-UP EXERCISES – Quick Overview

10. Creating space for ascending line

11. Martellato

12. Marcato; Upward leaps on the breath

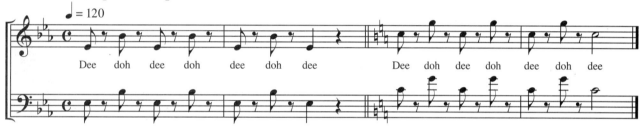

13. Upward leaps on the breath, with line; Listening

14. Range extension upward

CHORAL WARM-UP EXERCISES – Quick Overview

15. Range consistency with upward and downward leaps

16. Upward leaps on the breath; with line

17. Making space on upward leap; Vowel modification

18. Range extension

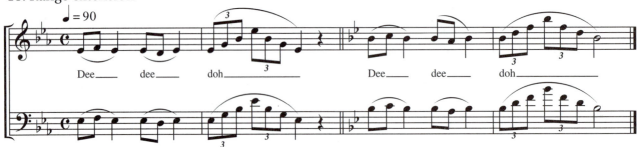

19. Martellato

CHORAL WARM-UP EXERCISES – Quick Overview

CHORAL WARM-UP EXERCISES WITH ACCOMPANIMENTS

#1
Legato; Line
CD Tracks 1 & 2

Acc. Marilyn Shenenberger

250

#1 Legato; Line

This page intentionally left blank.

#2
Repeated Tone with Crescendo & Decrescendo
CD Tracks 3 & 4

Acc. Marilyn Shenenberger

#3
Maintain Spacious, High, & Forward in Low Register
CD Tracks 5 & 6

Acc. Marilyn Shenenberger

#3 Maintain Spacious, High, & Forward in Low Register

This page intentionally left blank.

#4
Legato at Slow Tempo
CD Tracks 7 & 8

#5
Singing on Breath through Moving Eighth Notes
CD Tracks 9 & 10

Acc. Marilyn Shenenberger

#5 Sing on Breath through Moving Eighth Notes

#6
Register Consistency with Downward Leaps
CD Tracks 11 & 12

Acc. Marilyn Shenenberger

#6 Register Consistency with Downward Leaps

#7
Range Extension Downward
CD Tracks 13 & 14

Acc. Marilyn Shenenberger

#7 Range Extension Downward

#8
Range Extension Downward
CD Tracks 15 & 16

Acc. Marilyn Shenenberger

#8 Range Extension Downward

265

#9
Range Extension Upward and Maintaining On-the-Breath Singing
CD Tracks 17 & 18

Acc. Marilyn Shenenberger

#9 Range Extension Upward and Maintaining On-the-Breath Singing

#9 Range Extension Upward and Maintaining On-the-Breath Singing

This page intentionally left blank.

#10
Creating Space for Ascending Line
CD Tracks 19 & 20

Acc. Marilyn Shenenberger

#10 Creating Space for Ascending Line

#11
Martellato
CD Tracks 21 & 22

Acc. Marilyn Shenenberger

#11 Martellato

#12
Marcato; Upward Leaps on Breath
CD Tracks 23 & 24

Acc. Marilyn Shenenberger

#12 Marcato; Upward Leaps on Breath

#13
Upward Leaps on the Breath, with Line; Listening
CD Tracks 25 & 26

#13 Upward Leaps on the Breath, with Line; Listening

#13 Upward Leaps on the Breath, with Line; Listening

#14
Range Extension Upward
CD Tracks 27 & 28

Acc. Marilyn Shenenberger

#14 Range Extension Upward

#14 Range Extension Upward

281

#15
Range Consistency with Upward & Downward Leaps
CD Tracks 29 & 30

Acc. Marilyn Shenenberger

282

#15 Range Consistency with Upward & Downward Leaps

#16
Upward Leaps on the Breath, with Line
CD Tracks 31 & 32

Acc. Marilyn Shenenberger

#16 Upward Leaps on the Breath, with Line

#17
Making Space on Upward Leap, Vowel Modification
CD Tracks 33 & 34

Acc. Marilyn Shenenberger

286

#17 Making Space on Upward Leap, Vowel Modification

#18
Range Extension
CD Tracks 35 & 36

Acc. Marilyn Shenenberger

#18 Range Extension

289

#19
Martellato
CD Tracks 37 & 38

Acc. Marilyn Shenenberger

#19 Martellato

#20
Range Extension
CD Tracks 39 & 40

Acc. Marilyn Shenenberger

#20 Range Extension

#20 Range Extension

This page intentionally left blank.

#21
Teaching Martellato Exercise
Begin at 60; Increase Tempo
Follow Instructions in Choral Ensemble Warm-Up Text
CD Tracks 41 & 42

Acc. Marilyn Shenenberger

* The 10th chord may be rolled if it is beyond the accessible reach of the accompanist.

#21 Teaching Martellato Exercise

#22
Mixolydian Line with Crescendo and Decrescendo
CD Tracks 43 & 44

Acc. Marilyn Shenenberger

#22 Mixolydian Line with Crescendo and Decrescendo

#23
Aeolian Line and
Legato at Slow Tempo
CD Tracks 45 & 46

Acc. Marilyn Shenenberger

#23 Aeolian Line and Legato at Slow Tempo

#24
Aeolian Range Extension
CD Tracks 47 & 48

Acc. Marilyn Shenenberger

#24 Aeolian Range Extension

303

RECORDING ARTISTS

MARILYN SHENENBERGER has worked closely with James Jordan for the past four years, and has been an integral part of Dr. Jordan's work in the teaching of Choral Ensemble Intonation. She is featured on the Choral Ensemble Intonation Video, and is co-author with Dr. Jordan of *Ear Training: Aural Immersion Exercises for Choirs*, a book which provides both printed and recorded piano accompaniments for intonation exercises and choral warm-ups in eight modes including octatonic as well as major and minor keys. Marilyn has a master's in choral conducting from Westminster Choir College, Dalcroze teaching certificate from the Dalcroze School of Music in Manhattan, and has served as accompanist for a variety of vocal and instrumental soloists, and choral ensembles, here and in Europe, most recently accompanying for cellist Robert Cafaro, heard on this recording, and bass player Ranaan Meyer, Curtis Alumni Fellowship recipient. On the Westminster Campus, she has accompanied for Dr. James Jordan, Dr. Andrew Megill, and Dr. Joseph Flummerfelt. In addition to accompanying, Marilyn is Director of Music at Faith United Presbyterian Church in Medford, NJ, where she is the organist and director of three handbell choirs, a children's choir, two youth choirs, and an adult choir.

DAWN WILLIAMS is the orchestral contractor and music editor for NFL Films by day, and flautist by night. She has played with the Tallahassee Chamber Orchestra, and in the greater Philadelphia area, performs regularly with Trio Classica, and Bel Canto Chamber Music Ensemble. Since purchasing her rose gold flute a year ago, she has appeared as soloist with several ensembles locally, but this is the first recording with the Aurumite Powell flute.

ROBERT CAFARO is a graduate of Juilliard with Bachelor and Master of Music degrees. After graduation, he played chamber music full time and served on the faculty of the University of Virginia until 1983, when he performed regularly with the Metropolitan Opera Orchestra. He later joined the Baltimore Symphony, and in 1985 became a member of the Philadelphia Orchestra. Mr. Cafaro is an avid soloist and chamber musician; he has performed recitals and appeared as soloist in major cities of the world. An active teacher as well, he has been on the cello faculty of the Philadelphia College of Bible, College of NJ, Hartwick Summer Festival in Oneonta, NY, and the Summer Strings Seminar in Rhinebeck, NY.

KATHARINE FREDERICK, sound engineer, is a senior at Temple University. Her studio training began at Lebanon Valley College, where she was Studio Recording Manager, and Sound Technician for the Annual Spring Arts Festivals. Her internship with National Public Radio included editing experience as production assistant, and most recently, she has mastered the recording which accompanies *Ear Training: Aural Immersion Exercises for Choirs* by Dr. Jordan & Marilyn Shenenberger. She is currently Marketing Director for Billy Stott Productions in the tri-state area.

PART XI

THE CHORAL WARM-UP
TEACHING CARDS
AND CORE
VOCAL EXERCISES

For quick and easy reference, the **Teaching Cards** presented throughout this book have been reproduced as note cards, available separately from the publisher (GIA, G-63971). They are concise duplications of the pedagogical materials presented in each chapter, designed for use in rehearsals as pedagogical "reminders."

The Choral Warm-Up Teaching Cards

The Fourteen Pedagogical Cardinal Rules   (pp. 9-10)
Choral Ensemble Pedagogical Hierarchy   (p. 28)
Deconstruction of Posture Brought into the Rehearsal   (p. 35)
Six Points of Skeletal Balance   (p. 45)
Verbal Alignment Cues for Rehearsal   (p. 48)
Teaching Procedure for the Downward Sigh   (p. 50)
Finding the "Cave"   (p. 51)
Verbal Cues for Inhalation and Exhalation   (pp. 62-63)
Humming and Chewing: Resonance-Generating Exercises   (p. 74)
Developing Specific Resonances   (p. 75)
Teaching the "oo" Vowel   (p. 83)
Teaching the "ee" Vowel   (p. 83)
Teaching Dynamics   (p. 88)
Steps for Teaching Crescendo/Decrescendo   (pp. 89-90)
Steps for Teaching Upward Range Extension   (pp. 92-93)
Steps for Teaching Downward Range Extension   (p. 94)
Teaching Procedure for Leaps   (pp. 94-95)
Note Grouping Rules for Internal Musical Phrasing   (pp. 95-96)
Techniques for Teaching and Reinforcing Legato Line   (p. 97)
Teaching Procedure for Pointing for Martellato and Textural Clarification   (p. 100)
Teaching Procedure for Martellato   (p. 102)
Steps for Choosing Appropriate Diction Vowel Color   (p. 103)
Order of Vowel and Consonant Correction   (p. 107)
Teaching Schwas   (p. 110)
Movement Coordination Sequence   (p. 196)

Additionally, the melodies for all of the **Core Vocal Exercises** are reproduced on reference cards, available separately from the publisher (GIA, G-63971), for easy access and use in the warm-up.

Core Vocal Exercises

Exercise 1: Legato; Line
Exercise 2: Repeated Tone with Crescendo and Decrescendo
Exercise 3: Maintain SHF (Spacious, High, and Forward) in Low Register
Exercise 4: Legato at a Slow Tempo
Exercise 5: Singing on Breath through Moving Eighth Notes
Exercise 6: Register Consistency with Downward Leaps
Exercise 7: Range Extension Downward (Descends Chromatically)
Exercise 8: Range Extension Downward (Descends Chromatically)
Exercise 9: Range Extension Upward and Maintaining On-the-Breath Singing
Exercise 10: Creating Space for Ascending Line
Exercise 11: Martellato
Exercise 12: Marcato; Upward Leaps on the Breath
Exercise 13: Upward Leaps on the Breath, with Line; Listening
Exercise 14: Range Extension Upward
Exercise 15: Range Consistency with Upward and Downward Leaps
Exercise 16: Upward Leaps on the Breath; with Line
Exercise 17: Making Space on Upward Leap; Vowel Modification
Exercise 18: Range Extension
Exercise 19: Martellato
Exercise 20: Range Extension
Exercise 21: Teaching Martellato
Exercise 22: Mixolydian Line with Crescendo and Decrescendo
Exercise 23: Aeolian Line and Legato at Slow Tempo
Exercise 24: Aeolian Range Extension

Bibliography and Resource List

Aaron, J. "A study of the effects of vocal coordination on pitch accuracy, range, pitch discrimination, and tonal memory of inaccurate singers." Ph.D. dissertation. The University of Iowa, 1990.

Adler, Kurt. *Phonetics and Diction in Singing.* Minneapolis, MN: University of Minnesota Press, 1967.

Agostini, Emilo. "Diaphragm activity in breath holding: factors relating to onset." *Journal of Applied Physiology,* 18, 1963, pp. 30–36.

Andrews, Moya L., and Anne C. Summers. *Voice Therapy for Adolescents.* San Diego, CA: Singular Publishing Group, 1991.

Appelman, D. Ralph. "Science of Resonance." *Music Journal,* 17, 1959, pp. 44–45.

—. *The Science of Vocal Pedagogy.* Bloomington, IN: Indiana University Press, 1967.

Archibeque, Charlene. "Making Rehearsal Time Count." *The Choral Journal,* September 1992, pp. 18–19.

Armstrong, Kerchal, and Donald Hustad. *Choral Musicianship and Voice Training: An Introduction.* Carol Stream, IL: Somerset Press, 1986.

Baer, Hermanus. " Establishing a correct basic technique for singing." *The NATS Bulletin,* 28, 1972, pp. 12–14.

Baldwin, James. "Some Techniques for Achieving Better Choral Tone through Vowel Purity." *The Choral Journal,* September, 1985, pp. 5–12.

Barlow, W. The Alexander Technique. New York: Alfred A Knopf, 1973.

Bassini, Carlo. *Bassini's Art of Singing: An Analytical and Physiological System for the Cultivation of the Voice.* Boston, MA: Oliver Ditson and Co., 1857.

Bergman, Leola Nelson. *Music Master of the Middle West: The Story of F. Melius Christiansen and the St. Olaf Choir.* New York: Da Capo Press, 1968.

Bertalot, John. *5 Wheels to Successful Sight Reading.* Minneapolis, MN: Augsburg Fortress, 1993.

———. *Immediately Practical Tips for Choral Directors.* Minneapolis, MN: Augsburg Fortress, 2003.

Bertaux, B. "Teaching Children of All Ages to Use the Singing Voice, and How to Work with Out-of-Tune Singers." In Darrel Walters and Cynthia Taggart. Readings in *Music Learning Theory.* Chicago: GIA Publications, pp. 92–104.

Bloom, Benjamin. *Stability and Change in Human Characteristics.* New York: Wiley, 1964.

Bollew, Jospeh A. "Is falsetto false?" *The Etude,* July, 1954, p. 14.

Boone, D. R. *The Voice and Voice Therapy.* Englewood Cliffs, NJ: Prentice-Hall, 1977.

Bouhuys, Arend. *The Physiology of Breathing.* London: Gruene and Stratton, 1977.

Bradley, M. "Prevention and correction of vocal disorders in singers." *The NATS Bulletin,* May/June, 1980, p. 39.

Bravender, Paul E. "The Effect of Cheerleading on the female singing voice." *The NATS Bulletin,* 37, 1980, p. 39.

Brodnitz, Friedrich. "On Change of Voice." *The NATS Bulletin,* 40, 1984, pp. 24–26.

Brown, Ralph Morse. *The Singing Voice.* New York: Macmillan Co., 1946.

Brown, William Earl. *Vocal Wisdom: Maxims of Giovanni Battista Lamperti.* Enlarged Edition. Boston, MA: Crescendo Publishers, 1973.

Bunch, Meribeth. *Dynamics of the Singing Voice.* New York: Springer-Verlag, 1982.

Burgin, John Carroll. *Teaching Singing.* Metuchen, NJ: Scarecrow Press, 1973.

Campbell, Don G. *Master Teacher: Nadia Boulanger.* Washington, DC: The Pastoral Press, 1984.

Christy, Van A. *Expressive Singing.* Dubuque, IA: William C. Brown and Co., 1974.

———. *Foundations in Singing.* Dubuque, IA: William C. Brown and Co., 1976.

Clippinger, David Alva. *The Head Voice and Other Problems.* Boston, MA: Oliver Ditson, 1917.

Coffin, Berton. "The Instrumental Resonance of the Singing Voice." *The NATS Bulletin,* 31, 1974, pp. 26–39.

——. "The Relationship of Breath, Phonation and Resonance in Singing." *The NATS Bulletin,* 31, 1975, pp. 18–24.

Collins, D. L. *The Cambiata Concept.* Arkansas: The Cambiata Press, 1981.

Colwell, Richard. *The Evaluation of Music Teaching Learning.* Englewood Cliffs, NJ: Prentice-Hall, 1970.

Cooksey, John M. "Development of a Contemporary, Eclectic Theory for the Training and Cultivation of the High School Male Changing Voice." *The Choral Journal,* October 1977.

——. "Development of a Contemporary, Eclectic Theory for the Training and Cultivation of the High School Male Changing Voice, Part II: Scientific and Empirical Findings; Some Tentative Solutions." *The Choral Journal,* October 1977, pp. 12–14.

——. "Development of a Contemporary, Eclectic Theory for the Training and Cultivation of the High School Male Changing Voice, Part III: Developing an Integrated Approach to the Care and Training of the Junior High School Male Changing Voice." *The Choral Journal,* October 1977, pp. 7–9.

——. "Development of a Contemporary, Eclectic Theory for the Training and Cultivation of the Junior High School Male Changing Voice. *The Choral Journal,* 18, October 1977 and January 1978.

Cooper, Morton. "Vocal Suicide in Singers." *The NATS Bulletin,* 16, 1970, p. 31.

Corbin, Lynn A. "Practical Applications of Vocal Pedagogy for Choral Ensembles." *The Choral Journal,* March 1986, pp. 5–10.

Coward, Henry. *Choral Technique and Interpretation.* Salem, NH: Ayer Company Publishers, 1972.

Darrow, G. F. *Four Decades of Choral Training.* Metuchen, NJ: The Scarecrow Press, 1975.

Dart, Thurston. *The Interpretation of Music.* New York: Harper and Row, 1963.

Davison, Archibald T. *Choral Conducting.* Cambridge, MA: Harvard University Press, 1940.

Decker, Harold A., and Julius Herford. *Choral Conducting Symposium.* Englewood Cliffs, NJ: Prentice-Hall, 1988.

Demorest, Steven. "Customizing Choral Warm-Ups." *The Choral Journal,* February 1993, pp. 25–28.

——. "Structuring a Musical Choral Rehearsal." *Music Educators Journal,* January 1996, p. 25.

Donaldson, Robert P. "The Practice and Pedagogy of Vocal Legato." *The NATS Bulletin,* 29, 1973, pp. 12–21.

Doscher, Barbara M. *The Functional Unity of the Singing Voice.* Metuchen, NJ: The Scarecrow Press, 1988.

Duarte, F. "The Principles of Alexander Technique Applied to Singing: The Significance of the Preparatory Set." *Journal of Research in Singing,* 5–1, pp. 3–21.

Ehmann, Wilhelm, and Frauke Haasemann. *Voice Building for Choirs.* Chapel Hill, NC: Hinshaw Music, Inc., 1982.

Ehmann, Wilhelm. *Choral Directing.* Minneapolis, MN: Augsburg Publishing House, 1968.

——. "Performance Practice of Bach's Motets." *American Choral Review,* VII, September 1964, 4–5, and December 1964, 6–7, and March 1965, 6, and June 1965, 8–12.

Eichenberger, Rodney. *What You See Is What You Get.* (Video) Chapel Hill, NC: Hinshaw Music, Inc.

Ericson, Eric. *Choral Conducting.* New York: Walton Music Corporation, 1976.

Feder, R. J. "Vocal Health: A View from the Medical Profession." *The Choral Journal,* 30–7, pp. 23–25.

Finn, William J. *The Art of the Choral Conductor.* Volumes I and II. Evanston, IL: Summy-Birchard Company, 1960.

——. *The Conductor Raises His Baton.* New York: Harper and Brothers, 1944.

Fisher, R. E. "Choral Diction with a Phonological Foundation." *The Choral Journal,* 27–5, pp. 13–18.

Fowler, Charles (Ed.). *Conscience of a Profession: Howard Swan.* Chapel Hill, NC: Hinshaw Music, Inc., 1987.

Frisell, Anthony. *The Baritone Voice.* Boston: Crescendo Publishers, 1972.

——. *The Soprano Voice.* Boston: Bruce Humphries, 1966.

——. *The Tenor Voice.* Boston: Bruce Humphries, 1964.

Fuchs, Peter Paul. *The Psychology of Conducting.* New York: MCA, 1969.

Fuchs, Viktor. *The Art of Singing and Voice Technique.* New York: London House and Maxwell, 1964.

Gackle, Lynn. "The Adolescent Female Voice: Characteristics of Change and Stages of Development." *The Choral Journal,* 31–8, pp. 17–25.

Gajard, Dom Joseph. *The Solesmes Method.* Collegeville, MN: The Liturgical Press, 1960.

Garcia, Manuel. *A Complete Treatise on the Art of Singing.* Trans. Donald V. Paschke. New York: Da Capo Press, 1972.

Garretson, Robert L. "The Singer's Posture and the Circulatory System." *The Choral Journal,* April, 1990, p. 19.

Glenn, Carole (Ed.). *In Quest of Answers: Interviews with American Choral Conductors.* Chapel Hill, NC: Hinshaw Music, Inc., 1991.

Goetze, Mary. "Factors Affecting Accuracy in Children's Singing." *Dissertation Abstracts International,* 46, 2955A.

Gordon, Edwin E. *Advanced Measures of Music Audiation.* Chicago: GIA Publications, 1989.

——. *Intermediate Measures of Music Audiation.* Chicago: GIA Publications, 1982.

——. Learning Sequences in Music. Chicago: GIA Publications, 1989.

——. *The Iowa Tests of Music Literacy.* GIA Publications, 1991.

———. *The Nature, Description, Measurement and Evaluation of Music Aptitudes.* Chicago: GIA Publications, 1987.

———. "Research Studies in Audiation:1," *Council for Research in Music Education,* 84, 1985, pp. 34–5.

Haasemann, Frauke, and Irene Willis. *Group Vocal Technique for Children's Choirs.* Unpublished manuscript.

Haasemann, Frauke, and James Jordan. *Group Vocal Technique.* Chapel Hill, NC: Hinshaw Music, 1991.

———. *Group Vocal Technique: The Vocalise Cards.* Chapel Hill, NC: Hinshaw Music, 1991.

———. *Group Vocal Technique.* (Video) Chapel Hill, NC: Hinshaw Music, 1991. *(This video is a wonderful teaching/learning tool that documents in film the teaching of Frauke Haasemann. It is highly recommended to all students of vocal technique for choirs.)*

Hisley, Philip D. "Head quality versus nasality: a review of pertinent literature." *The NATS Bulletin,* 28, 1971, pp. 4–15.

Hofbauer, Kurt. *Praxis der Chorsichen Stimmbildung.* Mainz: Schott Verlag, 1978.

Huff-Gackle, Lynne Martha. "The Adolescent Female Voice: Characteristics of Change and Stages of Development." *The Choral Journal,* pp. 31–38, 1991, March, pp. 17–25.

———. "The effect of selected vocal techniques for breath management, resonation, and vowel unification on tone production in the junior high school female voice." Ph.D. dissertation, University of Miami, 1987.

James, David. "Intonation problems at the level of the larynx." *The NATS Bulletin,* 39, 1983, pp. 14–16.

Jordan, James, and Marilyn Shenenberger. *Ear Training Immersion Exercises for Choirs.* Chicago: GIA Publications, 2004.

Jordan, James, and Matthew Mehaffey. *Choral Ensemble Intonation.* Chicago: GIA Publications, 2001.

Jordan, James. "Audiation and Sequencing: An Approach to Score Preparation." *The Choral Journal,* XXI/8, April 1981, pp. 11–13.

———. "Choral Intonation: A Pedagogical Problem for the Choral Conductor." *The Choral Journal,* April 1987.

———. *Evoking Sound: Fundamentals of Choral Conducting and Rehearsing.* Chicago: GIA Publications, 1996.

———. "False Blend: A Vocal Pedagogy Problem for the Choral Conductor." *The Choral Journal,* XXIV/10, June1984, pp. 25–26.

———. *The Musician's Soul.* Chicago: GIA Publications, 1999.

———. *The Musician's Spirit.* Chicago: GIA Publications, 2002.

———. "Toward a Flexible Sound Ideal Through Conducting: Some Reactions to Study with Wilhelm Ehmann." *The Choral Journal,* XXV/3, November 1984, pp. 5–6.

———. *Learn Conducting Technique With the Swiss Exercise Ball.* Chicago: GIA Publications, 2004.

Joyner, D. R. "The Monotone Problem." *Journal of Research in Music Education,* 17-1, pp. 114–125.

Judd, Percey. *Vocal Technique.* London: Sylvan Press, 1951.

Kagen, Sergius. *On Studying Singing.* New York: Dover Publications, 1960.

Keenze, Marvin H. "Singing City Choirs." T*he Journal of Church Music,* X,* *September 1968, pp. 8–10.

Kemp, Helen. *Of Primary Importance.* Garland, TX: The Choristers Guild, 1989.

Kirk, Theron. Choral Tone and Technique. Westbury, NY: Pro-Art, 1956.

Klein, Joseph J. *Singing Technique: How to Avoid Vocal Trouble.* Princeton, NJ: D. VanNostrand, 1967.

Lamperti, Francesco. *The Technics of Bel Canto.* New York: G. Schirmer, 1905.

Lamperti, Giovanni Battista. *Vocal Wisdom.* New York: Taplinger Publishing Company, 1957.

Landeau, Michael. "Voice Classification." *The NATS Bulletin,* October 1963, pp. 4–8.

Large, John, Edward Baird, and Timothy Jenkins. "Studies of Male Voice Mechanisms: Preliminary Report and Definition of the term 'Register.'" *Journal of Research in Singing,* 4, 1981, pp. 1–26.

Lieberman, Phillip. *Intonation, Perception and Language.* Cambridge, MA: The MIT Press, 1967.

Mari, Nanda. *Canto e voce.* Milan: G Ricordi, 1970.

Marshall, Madeleine. The Singer's Manual of English Diction. New York: G. Schirmer, 1963.

Mason, Lowell. Manual of the Boston Academy of Music for Instruction. *In the Elements of Vocal Music on the System of Pestalozzi.* Boston, MA: J. H. Wilkins and R. B. Carfter, 1839.

McKinney, James. *The Diagnosis and Correction of Vocal Faults.* Nashville, TN: Broadman Press, 1982.

Moe, Daniel. *Basic Choral Concepts.* Minneapolis, MN: Augsburg, 1968.

Moriarty, John. *Diction: Italian, Latin, French and German.* Boston, MA: E. C. Schirmer, 1975.

Miller, Kenneth C. *Principles of Singing.* Englewood Cliffs, NJ: Prentice Hall, 1983.

Miller, Richard. "The Solo Singer in the Choral Ensemble." *The Choral Journal,* March 1995.

——. *On the Art of Singing.* New York: Oxford, 1996.

——. *English, French, German and Italian Techniques of Singing.* Metuchen, NJ: Scarecrow Press, 1977.

——. *The Structure of Singing.* New York: Schirmer Books, 1986.

——. *Training Soprano Voices.* New York: Oxford University Press, 2000.

——. *Training Tenor Voices.* New York: Schirmer Books, 1993.

Montini, Nicola A. *The Correct Pronunciation of Latin According to Roman Usage.* Chicago: GIA Publications, 1973.

Phillips, Kenneth H. "The Effects of Group Breath Control Training on Selected Vocal Measures Related to the Singing Ability of Children in Grades Two, Three and Four." Ph.D. dissertation. Kent State University, 1983.

Proctor, Donald. *Breathing, Speech and Song.* New York: Springer-Verlag, 1980.

Pysh, Gregory M. "Chorophony: The Art of Father Finn." *The Choral Journal,* November 1996, p. 37.

Rao, Doreen. *Choral Music Experience,* Vol. I: Artistry in Music Education. New York: Boosey and Hawkes, 1987.

———. *Choral Music Experience, Vol. 2: The Young Singing Voice.* New York: Boosey and Hawkes, 1987.

Reid, Cornelius L. *The Free Voice: A Guide to Natural Singing.* New York: Joseph Patelson Music House, 1965.

———. *Voice: Psyche and Soma.* New York: Joseph Patelson Music House, 1965.

Roberts, E., and A. Davies. "The Response of 'Monotones' to a Program of Remedial Training," *Journal of Research in Music Education,* 1975, 23, 4, pp. 227–239.

Robinson, Ray. "Wilhelm Ehmann's Approach to Choral Training." *The Choral Journal,* November 1984, pp. 5–7.

Robinson, R., and A. Winold. *The Choral Experience.* New York: Harper's College Press, 1976.

Rose, Arnold. *The Singer and the Voice.* New York: St. Martin's Press, 1971.

Rushmore, Robert. *The Singing Voice.* New York: Dodd and Mead, 1971.

Sable, Barbara Kinsey. *The Vocal Sound.* Englewood Cliffs, NJ: Prentice-Hall, Inc., 1982.

Sataloff, Robert Thayer, and J. R. Spiegel. "The Young Voice." *The NATS Journal,* 45 (3) 1989, p. 35–37.

Sataloff, Robert Thayer. *Professional Voice: The Science and Art of Clinical Care.* San Diego, CA: Singular Publishing Group, 1997.

——. "Ten Good Ways to Abuse Your Voice: A Singer's Guide to a Short Career. *The NATS Journal,* Part 1, 42–1, pp. 23–25.

——. "Ten Good Ways to Abuse Your Voice: A Singer's Guide to a Short Career. *The NATS Journal,* Part 2, 43–1, pp. 22–26.

——. *Vocal Health and Pedagogy.* San Diego, CA: Singular Publishing Group, 1998.

——. *Voice Perspectives.* San Diego, CA: Singular Publishing Group, 1998.

Seashore, Carl E. *The Psychology of Musical Talent.* Boston: Silver-Burdett, 1919.

Sellars-Young, Barbara. *Breathing Movement Exploration.* New York: Applause Books, 2001.

Scott, Anthony. "Acoustic Peculiarities of Head Tone and Falsetto." *The NATS Bulletin,* 33, 1974, pp. 32–35.

Shaw, Robert. "Letters to a Symphony Chorus." *The Choral Journal.* April, 1986, pp. 5–8.

Shuter-Dyson, Rosamund, and Gabriel Clive. *The Psychology of Musical Ability.* London: Methuen, 1981.

Stransky, J., and R. B. Stone. *Joy in the Life of Your Body.* New York: Beaufort, 1981.

Sundberg, Johann. *The Science of the Singing Voice.* DeKalb, IL: Northern Illinois University Press, 1987.

Sunderman, Lloyd Frederick. *Artistic Singing: Its Tone Production and Basic Understandings.* Metuchen, NJ: Scarecrow Press, Inc., 1970.

Swanson, Frederick J. "The Changing Voice." *The Choral Journal,* March 1976, pp. 5–14.

——. *The Male Singing Voice Ages Eight to Eighteen.* Cedar Rapids, IA: Laurence Press, 1977.

Swears, Linda. *Teaching the Elementary School Chorus.* West Nyack, NY: Parker, 1985.

Taff, Merle E. "An Acoustic Study of Vowel Modification and Register Transition in the Male Singing Voice." *The NATS Bulletin,* 22, 1965, pp. 8–35.

Taggart, Cynthia Crump. "The Measurement and Evaluation of Music Aptitudes and Achievement." In *Source Readings in Music Learning Theory.* Darrel Walters and Cynthia Crump Taggart (Eds.) Chicago: GIA Publications, 1989, pp. 45–55.

Thomas, Franz. *Bel Canto.* Berlin: George Achterberg Verlag, 1968.

Thomas, Kurt. *The Choral Conductor.* New York: Associated Music Publishers, 1971.

Thornton, Tony. *The Choral Singer's Survival Guide.* Los Angeles, CA: Vocal Planet Publishing, 2005.

Treash, Leonard. "The Importance of Vowel Sounds and Their Modification in Producing Good Tone." *The NATS Bulletin,* 4, 1943, p. 3.

Thurmond, James Morgan. *Note Grouping.* Camp Hill, PA: JMT Publications, 1989.

Vennard, William. *Developing Voices.* New York: Carl Fischer, Inc., 1973.

—. *Singing: The Mechanism and the Technic.* Revised edition. New York: Carl Fischer, Inc., 1967.

Waengler, Hans Heinrich. "Some Remarks and Observations on the Function of the Soft Palate." *The NATS Bulletin.* 25, 1968, p. 24.

Wall, Joan. *Diction for Singers.* Dallas, TX: Pst..., Inc, 1990.

—. International Phonetic Alphabet for Singers. Dallas, TX: Pst..., Inc. 1989.

Waring, F. *Tone Syllables.* Delaware Water Gap, PA: Shawnee Press, 1951.

Weikart, Phyllis. *Teaching Movement and Dance: A Sequential Approach to Rhythmic Movement.* Yipsilanti, MI: High Scope Press, 1989.

Webb, Guy (Ed). *Up Front!* Boston, MA: E. C. Schirmer, 1994.

Williamson, John Finley. "Choral Singing" (articles individually titled. Twelve articles in Etude, LXVIII and LXIX (April 1950–October 1951).

—. "Training the Individual Voice through Choral Singing." Proceedings of the Music *Teachers National Association,* XXXIII, 1938, pp. 52–59.

Wright, E. *Basic Choir Training.* Croydon, England: The Royal School of Church Music, 1955.

Zemlin, Willard R. *Speech and Hearing Science.* Englewood Cliffs, NJ: Prentice Hall, Inc., 1988.

Text Translation Resources

Jeffers, Ron. *Translations and Annotations of Sacred Latin Texts.* Corvalis, OR: Earthsongs, 1988.

Jeffers, Ron. *Translations and Annotations of Sacred German Texts.* Corvalis, OR: 1996.

Body Mapping Resources

Conable, Barbara, and William Conable. *How to Learn the Alexander Technique: A Manual for Students.* Portland, OR: Andover Press, 1995.

Conable, Barbara. *The Structures and Movement of Breathing.* Chicago: GIA Publications, 2000.

Conable, Barbara. *What Every Musician Needs to Know About the Body.* Portland, OR: Andover Press. *What Every Musician Needs to Know About the Body* is now available! It's a book about Body Mapping and the kinesthetic sense, and how they can be developed in ways that help musicians play well. It is full of information about the Alexander Technique, but it is very useful for people who don't have access to an Alexander teacher as well.

Vocal Technique and Choral Methods Resources: Books and Videos

Bartle, Jean Ashworth. *Lifeline for Children's Choir Directors.* Toronto: Gordon V. Thompson, 1988.

Blackstone, Jerry. *Working with Male Voices.* Video. Santa Barbara, CA: Santa Barbara Music.

Cooksey, John. *Working with Adolescent Voices.* St. Louis: CPH, 1999.

Dickson, John. "Score Study: A 'Magical Eye' for Musical Blueprints." *The Choral Journal* 39–8, March 1999, p. 9. *(Lengthy and detailed discussion of macro to micro score study, following model of Julius Herford and Margaret Hillis. Text is a primary consideration for this author. Academic and detailed, and very helpful.)*

Haasemann, Frauke, and James Jordan. *Group Vocal Technique.* Chapel Hill, NC: Hinshaw Music, Inc., 1991.

Haasemann, Frauke, and James Jordan. *Group Vocal Technique.* Video. Chapel Hill, NC: Hinshaw Music, Inc., 1989.

Haasemann, Frauke, and Jordan, James. *Group Vocal Technique: The Vocalise Cards.* Chapel Hill, NC: Hinshaw Music, Inc., 1990.

Horstmann, Sabine. *Chorische Stiimmbildung.* Merseburger Verlag, 1996. *(This small book contains many practical and useful exercises for use in constructing a warm-up.)*

Eichenberger, Rodney. *Enhancing Musicality through Movement.* Santa Barbara, CA: Santa Barbara Music.

Jordan, James, and Heather Buchanan. *Body Mapping and Basic Conducting Patterns.* Video and DVD. Chicago: GIA Publications, 2002.

Jordan, James, with Constantina Tsolainou, Craig Dennison, and Vincent Metallo. *The Choral Ensemble Warm-Up.* Chapel Hill, NC: Hinshaw Music, 1998.

Jordan, James. *Learn Conducting Technique With the Swiss Exercise Ball.* Chicago: GIA Publications, 2004.

Kemp, Helen. *Of Primary Importance.* Garland, TX: The Chorister's Guild, 1989.

Kemp, Helen. *A Helen Kemp Portrait: Insight and Inspiration from a Master Teacher of Children's Choirs.* Garland, TX: The Choristers Guild, 2001.

Leck, Henry. *The Boy's Changing Voice.* Video. Hal Leonard, Inc.

Miller, Richard. *The Structure of Singing.* New York: Schirmer Books, 1986.

Noble, Weston, and James Jordan. *Achieving Choral Blend through Standing Position.* Video. GIA Publications. In preparation (2005 release).

Phillips, Kenneth. *Teaching Kids to Sing.* New York: G. Schirmer, 1992.

Robinson, Russell. *Creative Rehearsal Techniques.* Video. Warner Brothers Music.

Shaw, Robert. *Preparing a Masterpiece, Volume I: The Brahms Requiem.* Video. New York: Carnegie Hall. *(Note: This valuable video contains a wonderful overview of Mr. Shaw's philosophies and rehearsal techniques. It is available only through the Carnegie Hall Gift Shop or carnegiehall.org.)*

Tsolainou, Constantina, and James Jordan. *Ensemble Diction.* Video. Chapel Hill, NC: Hinshaw Music, 1998.

Diction Resources

Cheek, Timothy. *Singing in Czech.* London: The Scarecrow Press, 2001.

Farish, Stephen. *French Diction for Singers.* Denton, TX: Gore Publishing Company, 1999.

Grubb, Thomas. *Singing in French.* New York: Schirmer, 1979.

Hines, Robert S. *Singer's Manual of Latin Diction and Phonetics.* London: Collier Macmillian Publishers, 1975.

Marshall, Madeleine. *The Singer's Manual of English Diction.* New York: G. Schirmer, 1963.

McGee, Timothy J. *Singing Early Music: The Pronunciation of European Languages in the Late Middle Ages and Renaissance.* Bloomington, IN: Indiana University Press, 1996.

Moriarty, John. *Diction: Italian, Latin, French and German.* Boston, MA: E. C. Schirmer, 1975.

Anatomical Model Resources

Anatomy.com. A company that markets anatomical models for use in Body Mapping instruction.

Aptitude Testing

Gordon, Edwin E. *Advanced Measures of Music Audiation.* Chicago: GIA Publications.

Gordon, Edwin E. *Intermediate Measures of Music Audiation.* Chicago: GIA Publications.

Gordon, Edwin E. *Primary Measures of Music Audiation.* Chicago: GIA Publications.

Web Sites

evokingsound.com Web site of James Jordan.

bodymap.org Web site of Barbara Conable.

giamusic.com Web site of GIA Publications (including Aptitude Tests).

hinshawmusic.com Web site of Hinshaw Music.

voiceinsideview.com This is the Web site for information concerning *Your Voice: An Inside View—Multimedia Voice Science and Pedagogy,* by Scott McCoy. This is a tremendous resource to assist in Body Mapping the vocal apparatus for your choir. The book, with its companion CD-ROM, is a multimedia exploration of voice science and pedagogy that is among the first pedagogical textbooks to make extensive use of audio, video, and high-resolution photographic examples. This is achieved through an interactive computer program designed to be used as a stand-alone application or in combination with a traditional printed text that references multimedia examples. The program runs directly from a CD-ROM.

Available for PC and MAC, the CD-ROM includes 150+ video examples, 85 audio examples, 100 photos and drawings, including images from the Netter Collection and the Rohen Atlas of Anatomy Roll-Over Identification of Anatomical Features (point the mouse to a structure, its name and function will pop up). The CD-ROM is available independently or combined with a print version of the textbook.

About the Authors

James Jordan is recognized and praised from many quarters in the musical world as one of the nations pre-eminent conductors, writers, and innovators in choral music. Having been called a "visionary" by *The Choral Journal,* his career and publications have been devoted to innovative educational changes in the choral art that have been embraced around the world. A master teacher, Dr. Jordan's pioneering writing and research concerning the use of Laban Movement Analysis for the teaching of conducting and movement to children has dramatically changed teaching in both of those disciplines. Called the "Father of the Case Study," he was the first researcher to bring forward the idea of the case study as a viable and valuable form of research for the training and education of teachers.

One of the country's most prolific writers on the subjects of the philosophy of music making and choral teaching, Dr. Jordan has produced ten major textbooks and several choral series bearing his name, and he has contributed to four other textbooks. In 2004, four new books authored by him will be published: *Learn Conducting Technique With the Swiss Exercise Ball, Ear Training Immersion Exercises for Choirs* (Conductor's Edition and Singer's Edition), *Evoking Sound: The Choral Ensemble Warm-Up* (book and Accompanist Supplement) and *The Musician's Walk* (all published by GIA Publications, Chicago). His books on the subject of Vocal Technique for Choirs are considered as essential for the education of conductors around the world. His choral conducting book, *Evoking Sound,* was named as a "must read" list of six books by *The Choral Journal.* His newest book, *Ear Training Immersion Exercises for Choirs* details the first comprehensive approach toward aural literacy for choirs using solfege and a unique system of score analysis that focuses on what is aurally perceived by the choir. His books The Musician's Soul (GIA, 2000) and *The Musician's Spirit* (GIA, 2002), acclaimed by both instrumental and choral conductors alike, have been credited with beginning a transformation on how music is taught both in ensembles and in the classroom through a process of humanizing and loving.

Dr. Jordan also serves as Executive Editor of the Evoking Sound Choral Series, also published by GIA Publications, Chicago. This series presents choral literature at the highest levels for high school and college choirs. In addition to new compositions by America's finest composers, the series also presents new editions of standard choral repertoire, edited with singers in mind. Also unique to this series are solfege editions that utilize Jordan's groundbreaking approach to the use of solfege in choral ensembles that uses accurate aural analysis as the basis of the approach.

Dr. Jordan teaches and conducts at Westminster Choir College of Rider University in Princeton, New Jersey, one of the foremost centers for the study and performance of choral music in the world. At Westminster, he is an associate professor of conducting. For the past twelve years, he has served as conductor of The Westminster Chapel Choir. In the fall of 2004, he will conduct one of Westminster's highly select touring choirs, a newly inaugurated ensemble, The Westminster Williamson Voices. This choir's mission is not only choral performance and recording at the highest levels, but to serve as an ensemble that employs unique and cutting-edge approaches to the choral rehearsal and choral performance. The ensemble will also have at its center a significant outreach to the musical world through workshops and residencies. The ensemble will specialize premiere significant contributions to the choral literature. The Westminster Williamson Voices is also involved in educational recordings of significant educational choral literature for the next five years for GIA Publications, which will culminate in the recording of approximately two hundred essential pieces of choral literature. In addition to his responsibilities at Westminster, Dr. Jordan is a Distinguished Visiting Professor of Music Education at West Chester State University in West Chester, Pennsylvania.

James Jordan has been the recipient of many awards for his contributions to the profession. He was named as Distinguished Choral Scholar at The University of Alberta. He was made an honorary member of Phi Mu Alpha Sinfonia in 2002 at Florida State University. Composer Morten Lauridsen dedicated a movement of his acclaimed *Mid-Winter Songs* to Dr. Jordan.

This year alone, Dr. Jordan will present over thirty keynote addresses and workshops around the world. Dr. Jordan's writings and professional activities are detailed on his website: **Evokingsound.com.**

Marilyn Shenenberger has worked closely with James Jordan at Westminster Choir College. She has been an integral part of Dr. Jordan's work in teaching *Choral Ensemble Intonation,* recently co-authoring *Ear Training Immersion Exercises for Choirs* (GIA, G-6429). She has provided aural awareness accompaniments for Dr. Jordan's Chapel Choirs, is featured on the *Choral Ensemble Intonation* video, and has presented these concepts as a clinician at seminars and summer workshops. Shenenberger received her master's degree in choral conducting from Westminster Choir College and holds a Dalcroze certificate from the Dalcroze School of Music in Manhattan under Robert Abramson, Anne Farber, and Ruth Alperson. She is a seasoned performer and has worked collaboratively with a variety of vocal and instrumental soloists, and choral ensembles, here and in Europe, most recently accompanying for cellist Robert Cafaro of the Philadelphia Orchestra. In addition to accompanying and performing chamber music, Shenenberger is the Director of Music at Faith United Presbyterian Church in Medford, New Jersey, where she is the organist and director of three handbell choirs, a children's choir, two youth choirs, and an adult choir.

Eric Kephart, Photographer

Eric Scott Kephart is a graduate of the Art Institute of Philadelphia. His career encompasses many diverse artistic interests, from fashion design to painting, photography, graphic design, and various genres of performance art. He is the owner/curator of ZONK ARTS Gallery in Philadelphia. The gallery, while specializing in the showcasing and promotion of emerging artists, has a significant community outreach to support artists in Philadelphia. As an artist, Kephart's current interests include modern pointillism. His photography can be seen in James Jordan's book, *The Musician's Spirit*. He is active in The Philadelphia Art Community through his volunteer work for such outreach organizations as Journey Home, Long Live the Arts Benefit for the South Street Renaissance Gallary, and ASIAC (Aids Services in the Asian Community). His work can be seen on his Web site: zonkarts.com.

Index

abandonment of vocal responsibility, 15, 22–23
accompaniments, use of, xxi
acoustic standing of the choir for blend
    alto in front arrangement, 124
    definition, 122
    procedure, 125–130
    quartet standing fallacies, 122
alignment
    alignment cues, 48
    definition of, 39
    no work is being done, 46
aural immersion
    importance of, 115–118
    pedagogical sequencing, 118
awareness, definition of, 136
awareness reminders, 47
awe and wonder, 137–138
Body Mapping, definition of, 39
body maps, 40, 45
breath kneading exercise, 63
cave, creating, 50
Choral Ensemble Warm-Up Teaching Cards, xxi
closing the vowel
    components of a healthy vowel sound, 77
    definition of, 77
    open vowel, definition of, 78
    wrapping lips around sound for closure, 77
consistent tempo
    teaching procedures, 201
    using metronome to teach communal tempo kinesthetic, 202
consistent terminology, use of, 31
consonants (for warm-up)
    first line, 84
    second line, 84
    slenderizing, 85
    never use, 85
core of the body, 41
Core Vocal Exercises
    complete core exercises as they appear in accompanist supplement, 250–305
    definition of, 16
    guidelines for accompanists, 242–244
    quick overview of all exercises, 245–249
    reasons for accompanied vs. unaccompanied exercises, 16, 237
    Teaching Cards, 309–312
    teaching procedures, 238
    voicing decisions for accompaniments, 241
core of warm-up, 8
creating space, 12
crescendo/decrescendo, teaching, 88–89
curved seating arrangements, p. 123
deconstructing posture, 10, 33, 35
diaphragm activity, 71

diction
    "l" problems, 111
    order of vowel correction, 107
    pitfalls, 109–112
    "r" problems, 111
    six-step diction teaching technique, 104–107
    teaching procedures, 101–107
diphthongs, definition of, 110
dominant function, 16
downward sigh
    correct quality, 56
    definition of, 50
dynamics, teaching, 87
"ee" vowel, teaching, 83
"ee" and "oo" vowels
    importance of, 50
    interdependence, 108–109
eight-handed breathing exercise, 63
energizing choral sound, 134
exhalate, 12
Finn, William J., xvi
focus, vocal, 30
folders, proper use of, 47
fourteen pedagogical rules, 9
generate resonance, 13
gestures to support vocal technique
    air spin, 90
harmonic context, definition of, 16, 114
head tone, definition of, 76
high and forward sound, reinforcement of, 53
high larynx, definition of, 18
human commitment to sound, 14
    teaching, 70
IMMA, 3
inclusive awareness, 11
inhalate, 12
inhalation and exhalation verbal cues, 62
internal musical impulse, 197
Laban, Rudolf von
    biography, 197
    efforts in combination, 182–189
    flow, weight, time, space; definitions of, 181–182
    movement imagery exercises, 190
    philosophical basis, 180
    use in teaching musical line, 189
leaps, teaching, 94
legato, teaching, 95
lip trills, dangers of, 71
lips
    correct body map of, 54
    lip tension, 79
low larynx, 17
martellato
    definition of, 98
    teaching, 99, 100–101

method, definition of, xxi, 27
metronome, use of to teach communal tempo, 202
movement coordination sequence, 196
muscle coordination development, 195
music aptitude
- definition of, 2
- developmental music aptitude, 3
- interpretation of aptitude scores, 4
- stabilized music aptitude, 4

musical issues with line, 81
normal illusion of good sound, 81
note grouping, 95
off-the-breath singing
- definition of, 69
- teaching, 69

on-the-breath singing
- definition of, 63
- teaching, 63–67

"oo" and "ee" vowels
- importance of, 50
- teaching, 83

open vowels, definition of, 78
pedagogical seesaw, 135
physical gestures to reinforce vocal technique
- body tip, 150
- breath anchor and diagonal space umbrella, 151
- breath kneading, 147
- congealing sound mixing gesture, 162
- consonant wisp gesture, 170
- dipping, 149
- drooping hands, 151
- finger toss into forehead, 144
- finger twirl, 151
- flick and lighten, 151
- forward ball toss, 148
- forward spin, 146
- hand dab, 159
- hand smoothing gesture, 160
- heel of hand on forehead, 143
- high and forward finger wand ("oo" magnet), 157
- importance of, 14, 56
- linguine pull gesture, 166
- pointing, 140
- resonance swimming cap peel, 151
- sound rolling gesture, 169
- toss open leg lift, 145
- tossing clap, 157
- up and over, 56, 142
- upward cheekbone brush, 168
- upward toss, 172

PMMA, 3
pointing, use of, 99
points of alignment, 42
purpose of the warm-up, 20
range extension upward
- realigning the body, 10
- teaching, 91

recipes, vocal technique, 29, 87–96
rehearsal room chairs, proper use of, 43

reinforcing pitch awareness, 15
relaxation, 33
resonance
- cool breath, use of, 75
- creating, 73
- generating, 13
- humming and chewing, 74
- round vowels, 75
- specific resonances, 74–75
- tall/narrow vowels, 75
- warm breath, use of, 75

rhythm
- layers of rhythm audiation, 199–200
- structure of, 197

rhythmic commitment, 136
rhythmically vital sounds, 14
round vowels, 75
schwa
- definition of, 109–110
- teaching, 110

seating
- importance of, 18, 122–133
- SHF (spacious, high and forward), 15

sigh, 12, 49
- teaching, 50
- use, 59

singing on the breath, 14
soft palate, 52
somatics, definition of, 40
siren, definition of and use, 59
staccato
- compromise teaching techniques, 98
- definition of, 97

stacking chairs for height, 44
starting pitch for warm-ups, 76
support
- definition of, 63
- teaching, 63–68

Swiss ball, use of in rehearsal room, 34
system is comfort, 17
tall/narrow vowels, 75
template for planning warm-ups, 17, 206
- model template, 208–212
- completed model template, 213–218

trachea, remapping, 61
transition from speaking to singing, 20
troubleshooting charts, 220–236
up and over, definition of, 46
- range extension, downward, definition of, 93
- range extension, upward, definition of, 92

verbal alignment cues, 48
vocal curricula, 33
vocal modeling, 33
vocal responsibility, 15
vocalic flow, definition of, 80, 96–97
vowel development hierarchy, 82
vowel modification, 92
wrapping lips around sound, definition of, 53